"If you live long enough and are willing to blaze trails in the process, setbacks and failure will be a part of your journey, it's inevitable. In *Finding God in Sin City* we find a powerful story of a woman who experienced both personal and professional setbacks and who not only learned from those experiences, but rose above them and redefined herself. As I know firsthand and have experienced myself, this is no small feat in Las Vegas. I am honored to have witnessed Lynette's journey — both the highs and the lows - for more than two decades now. I know many will be inspired by the many lessons of rediscovery found in her book."

**Jan Jones Blackhurst**
**Mayor of Las Vegas, 1991-1999**
**Executive Vice President,**
**Communications and Government Relations**
**Caesars Entertainment**

"*Finding God in Sin City* is a great book about success and lasting significance. She is transparent about her life as a Miss America Contestant and Politician. I voted for her in her Las Vegas career of public service and I'd vote for her again. In *Finding God in Sin City*, she writes of what matters most and how people in the forefront pay a price. This book demonstrates what God can do to a yielded life."

**Danny Daniels**
**Author, International Speaker, Las Vegas Media**
**Personality and Founder of the**
**"Role Model and Heroes Project"**

"A remarkable career of service through the law, seen through the lens of a uniquely passionate faith; these are parables for our age."

**Stephen M. Sheppard, JSD**
**Dean and Charles E. Cantu Distinguished Professor**
**St. Mary's University School of Law**

"As always, Lynette's story is a true inspiration to me as well as to so many other people. Lynette found a way to get to the masses that also need to follow God's path. All they have to do is read this book *Finding God in Sin City*. For those of us who have already hit rock bottom either through tragedy or bad choices know, the only way for us to be able to take that next step on our life is to look to God for guidance. It might not be an easy journey, but with his love we will find peace."

**Dana Phillips**
**CEO and Executive Director,**
**Miss Oregon Scholarship Programs**

"This is the story of a beautiful woman and a loving God. The woman finds God in her humanness and brokenness, and God simply fulfills the promises of the Scriptures. Now she is a powerful witness of how God changes lives and uses people to proclaim his message of love and forgiveness. As it has inspired me, it will inspire all those who are blessed to read it."

**LTC (Ret.) Vincent Burns,**
**U.S. Army Chaplain**

# Finding God in Sin City

A Woman's Journey, from Losing it All
to Discovering Life's True Riches

*Finding God in Sin City – A Woman's Journey, from Losing it All to Discovering Life's True Riches*

© 2015 by Lynette Boggs Quintanilla.

ISBN-10: 0-9907578-1-1
ISBN-13: 978-0-9907578-1-8

Interior photos by Sheila Lowe

*Printed in the United States of America.*

# Finding God in Sin City

A Woman's Journey, from Losing it All
to Discovering Life's True Riches

LYNETTE BOGGS QUINTANILLA

OVIEDO, FLORIDA

# Dedication

*I dedicate this book to my beautiful and unconditionally loving children, Adam and Rachel.*

# Contents

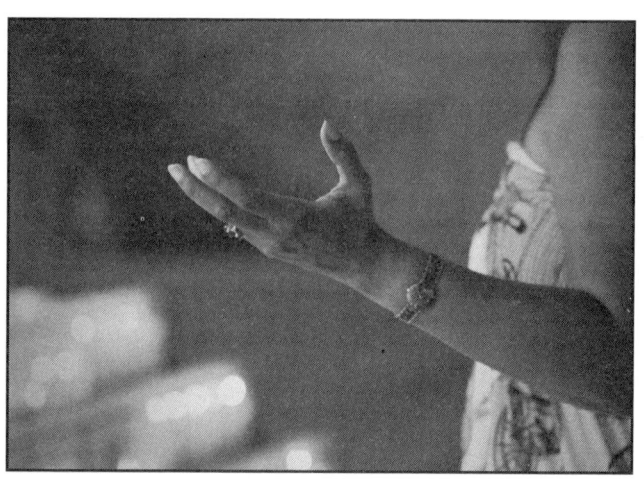

# Foreword

I t is hard to imagine a greater fall from grace than that of Lynette Boggs Quintanilla. It is even more difficult to imagine undergoing that fall while it is dissected in the public eye. In her book *"Finding God in Sin City,"* Lynette transforms her humbling and life-altering experience into nuggets of wisdom, which ultimately remind us that with faith in God, the impossible is possible. Her journey reinforces that the darkest periods in our lives can pave the way to the greater glory that God has in store for all of us.

To appreciate the person of faith that Lynette is today, one must understand the circumstances that brought her to this point in her life. Unless you lived in Las Vegas, Nevada, you would be hard pressed to know of the events that led to her downfall. I was vaguely aware of Lynette's legal troubles in Sin City. However, I had no idea of the extent of her problems, both criminal and marital. A former Miss Oregon who competed for the title of Miss America and a former Las Vegas City Councilwoman, Lynette describes the devastating impact that the felony charges and a divorce had on her life; a period of her life that was captured in the media, both print and television. Not only did she have to defend against charges that could have led to her imprisonment and taken her away from her children, the saga left her financially and emotionally drained.

As a reader, it is easy to imagine the pain and despair that Lynette must have felt from the financial devastation, and the loss of her marriage and political career. How humbling it must have been to go from the highs of walking across the stage in Atlantic City on national television, to earning six figures, to relying on a food pantry to feed her family. However, as Lynette explains, it is through those hardships that God tested her faith in Him. Although tempted, she did not disappoint Him. Each tale Lynette tells has a purpose. Her book provides an opportunity for the reader to grow spiritually. At the end of each chapter, she challenges the reader to examine his or her life for potential impediments to spiritual growth, whether it is to forgive the past transgression of another, or to let go of pride and shame.

I found myself moved by Lynette's journey, and amazed by her revelation that her challenges are still not over, despite overcoming many hurdles since leaving Las Vegas. If you are already a believer, this book will renew your faith in God. If you are in the depths of despair and feel that there is no hope, Lynette's words will uplift you and remind you that today's lows are tomorrow's highs, as long as you keep God by your side and believe in His promises.

**Marjorie Vincent-Tripp**
**Attorney**
**Miss America 1991**

# Introduction

Back in 2006, I believe a wager went down in Sin City between God and Satan. It went a little like this:

One day, the members of the heavenly court came to present themselves before the Lord, and the Accuser, Satan, came with them. "Where have you come from?" the Lord asked.

Satan answered the Lord, "I have been patrolling the earth, watching everything that's going on there, especially in Sin City. You know that what happens there stays there. Every stronghold I've ever created lives in abundance there."

Then the Lord asked Satan, "Have you noticed my servant, Lynette Boggs McDonald, the county commissioner? She is from a great family and highly educated. She fears me and stays away from evil."

"Yeah, yeah, yeah, but Boggs McDonald has good reason to worship you," Satan replied. "You have always put a wall of protection around her, her home, and her property. You have made her prosper in everything she does, from being crowned Miss Oregon to graduating from Notre

Dame, being elected an official, and having photographic kids and a husband. She was even featured in a Sunday edition of a George Will column and sits next to Senator John McCain at Naval Academy meetings. Look at how rich she is, but reach out and take away everything she has, and she will surely curse you to your face!"

"All right, then, you may test her," the Lord said to Satan. "Do whatever you want with everything she possesses, but don't harm her physically."

So, Satan left the Lord's presence. And all hell was unleashed on Lynette Boggs McDonald.

I am neither a pastor nor a theologian. I'm just a mother of two children who at one time appeared to have it all and then lost everything back in 2006. Out of desperation, frankly, I decided to try something pretty radical, at least for me. I decided to chase God. I chased Him like someone on fire runs for any water source. It was that kind of desperation.

*My test is now my testimony; my mess has become my message.*

I grew up in a Christian family and really can't remember missing a Sunday church service, but I never had a real, down-inside-my-marrow kind of relationship with God. In 2006, my marriage to my children's father ended and I was faced with criminal charges in Las Vegas for an allegation that no one in America has ever been feloniously charged with, an election violation for declaring an address in my election documents where my opponents said I didn't live.

What became the biggest setback of my life—professionally, psychologically, financially, and spiritually—turned into the greatest blessing of my life. My test is now my testimony; my mess has become my message. Everything I once considered a curse, I have used to bless others, especially the poor. I decided to write this book about the things God revealed to me during my chase after Him in Las Vegas, Nevada. Ironically, it happened in a place called Sin City, but it was where I learned most about God's grace.

I once heard someone say that your life may be the only Bible some people will ever read. This book is not intended to replace your Bible, but it is my hope that by sharing some of the things God revealed to me over the past seven years, and continues to reveal to me, you will be inspired to learn more about Jesus of Nazareth. You will learn that there isn't a situation you're facing that someone has not encountered before, and you will learn about the faithfulness of God. Just as importantly, you will learn how God uses and still needs rejected stones—those of us who have experienced failures, setbacks, mistakes, ridicule, and scorn—to advance His kingdom.

# Chapter 1

# A Rejected Stone

*I've come to pour my praise on Him*
*like oil from Mary's alabaster box*
*Don't be angry if I wash His feet with my tears*
*and dry them with my hair . . .*
—"Alabaster Box" written by Janice Sjostran and
made popular by recording artist Cece Winans

I have always considered myself a public servant. It's been the mantle I've worn at least since the age of twelve. Since I was once an elected official, many assume that being elected has always been my ultimate goal. It hasn't been and still isn't. Looking back, I can say I had as much joy in my heart when I was first allowed to lector a Mass at the age of twelve as when I won my first election that same year as the junior high student body vice president.

My propensity for service continued as my peers elected me their class president in my sophomore, junior, and senior years of high school. I was the captain of a girls' championship track team and was a member of gold-medal winning 4x100 and 4x400 relay teams. I was accepted to the University of Notre Dame and was a cheerleader for the Fighting Irish football and basketball teams. I personally know former NFL greats, such as Steve Beuerlein, Allen Pinkett, Mark Bavarro, Dave Duerson, and Heisman Trophy winner, Tim Brown. I cheered my heart out for them back in the day.

I am blessed with vocal talent, something one of my high school teachers, Cliff Burgeson, discovered when I was about fifteen. I was a vespers cantor at the Basilica of the Sacred Heart on Notre Dame's campus as an undergrad. A few years later, in 1989, as a graduate student at the University of Oregon, my vocal talents helped me win the Miss Oregon crown. I represented Oregon in the 1990 Miss America Pageant in Atlantic City, New Jersey. That year, Gretchen Carlson from Minnesota, now with Fox News, was the reigning Miss America. I have been a guest vocalist with the Las Vegas Philharmonic on more than one occasion.

A decade later, I became the first woman in Las Vegas history to represent a city council ward, representing Ward 2. Looking back, it almost seems impossible that it took almost until the end of the twentieth century for a woman to lead a ward. Jan Laverty Jones, who was elected mayor in 1991, was the first woman to break the gender barrier at Las Vegas City Hall, but I was the first woman of any race to ever be called "councilwoman."

Hoping to break another historical hurdle, I ran for the United States Congress in 2002 as the Republican candidate in Nevada's 1st Congressional District. A chance introduction in a Washington, DC, restaurant led to my becoming the subject of a Sunday editorial piece written by national columnist, George Will. During that campaign, former President George H. W. Bush hosted a campaign fundraiser to honor me and then-Congressman Jon Porter. I think we raised about $250,000 just that night for my campaign, thanks to the former president's support and presence.

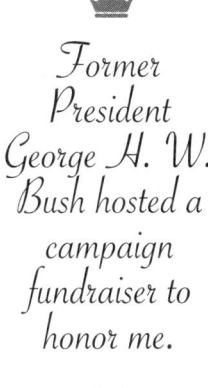

*Former President George H. W. Bush hosted a campaign fundraiser to honor me.*

After my five-year stint as city councilwoman, I pondered whether or not to ever run for office again. I felt I had accomplished all I was supposed to. I had opened beautiful community centers, numerous parks, and fire stations, and had added traffic lights to dangerous intersections. And God had answered a prayer that had lingered in my heart for many years. I was pregnant with my second child. After a failed pregnancy and several gynecological surgeries and procedures, God granted me a desire of my heart more than eight years after the birth of my precious son. I probably should have stopped at that point, hindsight being 20-20, but I didn't.

In 2004, my own county commissioner resigned from the Clark County Commission, leaving a vacancy that the governor of the state, the late Kenny Guinn, had to fill. My stepfather was a career soldier in the United States Army, and most of my childhood, until I was eighteen years old, was spent in Germany and Italy. My parents resided in Europe until 1996. Even as an adult, I would fly overseas to a military installation to visit my parents. I was taught that there were just certain people you never say no to when you're asked to serve. The president of the United States and military generals were always on top of that list for my family. Although I was never told this, I considered—and still do—a governor of a state to be held at that same level of respect and esteem. So, while I was driving home one March afternoon on the Summerlin Parkway and Governor Guinn called me to ask if I would consider resigning from the Las Vegas City Council to replace Mark James, I could give only one response, "Absolutely, sir!"

A few weeks after I gave birth to my daughter, the citizens of District F gave their stamp of approval to what had been an appointment by the governor by electing me outright as a Clark County Commissioner. On paper, I should not have won because I was a Republican in a district that had 10 percent more registered Democrats than Republicans. But I ran on my record of delivering services to the citizens and reminded voters of all the community centers, fire stations, and parks I had helped bring to their neighborhoods.

Since 80 percent of the entire state of Nevada resides in this one county, being elected to this particular body of government is considered extremely powerful, especially because there are only seventeen counties in Nevada. As a naturalized Texan today, my fellow Texans are blown away by this fact because there are 256 counties in the Lone Star state. There is no county in Texas (or anywhere else in America I'm aware of) that is as singularly dominant as Clark County, Nevada.

As an elected official, I, like every other office holder, had my political enemies. Although there are about six members of my own family who are members of the union, the Las Vegas Culinary Union hated my guts because I had once served on the Board of Directors of a gaming company that was nonunion, Station Casinos. The police hated me equally when I opposed the police union's push for a 40 percent pay raise on the heels of raising the sales tax a quarter of a cent. The sales tax increase had been pushed for the purpose of hiring more police officers. I was of the opinion that if salaries were raised that high, we would not be able to deliver on the promise made to voters when the sales tax was increased in 2004. I am sharing all of this for context. I'm personally a million miles from all the brouhaha and circumstances that led me to being indicted

*Like every other office holder, I had my political enemies.*

and eventually accepting an Alford plea after nearly two years of legal drama. To borrow a few legal terms, as far as I'm personally concerned, the past is relevant, but moot. I would not be walking in victory today if I had not gone through what I went through. Therefore, this book is not aimed to relive what happened to me. Its purpose is to share my rejoicing as I relive the many powerful lessons God showed me along the way. And one of the first lessons God showed me was that of the rejected stone.

As I was walking into the Clark County Regional Justice Center (RJC, as the locals call it) for the first time to face the accusations that had been made against me in the summer of 2007, something supernatural happened. The cornerstone of that multistory edifice became illuminated to me. It was as though the cornerstone was a marquee on the Las Vegas strip; it was radiating so brightly to me. It was, at that moment, that God revealed to me what even I had forgotten. My name was etched on the cornerstone of that courthouse, and not only there. God reminded me that my name was also on the cornerstones of hospitals, airport terminals, park monuments, fire stations, and on proclamations presented to hundreds upon hundreds of citizens and organizations. In that instant, I was reminded that I had been a cornerstone. And then I heard God speak, "Lynette, I was the *first* cornerstone, and the people rejected me, too, but I will give you a new name, just like I gave Peter, and the gates of hell will not prevail over you. Satan's victories are short-lived."

Although the media was salivating, hoping that I would

be hauled into court and they'd soon have mug shots and front-page stories, I kept listening to those words I had heard clearly in my spirit. When a local television reporter asked if I had anything to say, my only remarks were, "It's a beautiful day." It was because of what I had heard from Jesus as I was walking up the steps of the RJC.

You see, shortly before His death, crowds had gathered to cheer Jesus because they heard about all the miracles He had been performing. He didn't build parks and fire stations. What I did was chump change compared to things Jesus did in a three-year ministry. He made blind people see. He took two fish and five loaves and fed masses. He cast out demons and a woman who had such gynecological problems that she was bleeding for years was cured just by reaching for the hem of his garment. In the Bible, there is story after story after story of the miracles Jesus performed. He loved on people, especially those the world hated: prostitutes, lepers, and tax collectors, to name a few. One of the last big miracles He performed was raising His friend, Lazarus, from the dead. The report of this miracle spread like wildfire, and the people were lined up cheering with their palm branches, singing "Hosanna!" when Jesus came rolling into town on the back of a donkey.

*What I did was chump change compared to things Jesus did in a three-year ministry.*

As we know, His earthly ministry was only for a season. Before long, the people forgot all the good Jesus did; they just wanted Him dead. His political and spiritual enemies weren't going to stop until they accomplished that goal, and they did, as a matter of fact, accomplish their objective. They killed Jesus. They broke the cornerstone.

If you're reading this, it's possible you've been a rejected stone yourself. Perhaps the bank just foreclosed on your house, maybe you just got fired, or perhaps you fell off the wagon and are drinking again. You might be going through a divorce after twenty or thirty years of marriage (or twenty or thirty days). Perhaps you just went on a first date and were raped. For me, it was going through a public divorce and being charged in a court of law. I don't know what you're going through, but if you're broken, Satan is doing a victory dance at your expense.

Despite this, I want you to stick with me on this journey as I share with you the lessons I learned from the One who first overcame the entire world—Jesus of Nazareth, the first rejected stone. You see, what they did to Jesus was to try and stop the message. It almost worked. His apostles were so spooked and frightened from what they witnessed the Sanhedrin and Roman soldiers do to Jesus, that they ran into hiding. They were scared out of their minds that they would be next.

However, a crazy thing happened on the way to the tomb. You see, this huge boulder of a rock that was supposed to keep Him in, that bore the seal of the Roman government, and that was even guarded by a soldier, got moved. *Boom!* Although physically scarred and wounded, Jesus was alive. He was standing, hands and feet still pierced, with open wounds still on his body. Jesus' request to those first witnesses was to run and find the one who was probably in that upper room thinking about his own shortcomings and how he'd let everyone, especially Jesus, down. Jesus needed to see Peter. The one He had renamed from Simon (meaning "shifting sand") to Peter ("the rock"). Yes, Jesus needed the one who was a three-time turncoat, the one who freaked out on the boat during the storm—that same guy. It was this flawed and unreliable person Jesus intended to build His church upon.

You and I are as unreliable as Peter. God made us and, guess what? He knows all about our shortcomings. He still needs us. God needs us just like He needed Peter because the world is still messed up. Jesus didn't come here to die for perfect people with perfect lives. He came for those of us who have had jacked-up lives and experiences, often self-inflicted.

God needs us because the world is still hurting. It sounds cliché, but unless you've walked in someone else's moccasins, you really aren't going to speak with the same authority and authenticity as they can. God needs your mess to become a message for someone else. And because God has overcome Satan, so can we. Satan wants us to believe that when we've hit rock bottom, it's over. It isn't. That's a damn lie.

Seven years ago, I stood accused. Today, when I approach the bench, I stand as a licensed attorney and counselor at law. Yes, my enemies accomplished what they set out to do, but God had something else in mind—something bigger. God has put dreams in our heads and hearts. Satan is hoping you will give up on those dreams and the natural world is encouraging you to do just that, but God wants something greater for you.

What are you struggling with in your life right now? Do you have unresolved issues with your family, finances, career, friends, or health that eat at you constantly, fatigue you from worry, and make you want to give up? Don't give in to Satan's lie. Ask God what He wants you to learn from your trials and tribulations. Persevere through them. Call on your pastor, friends, and family members to help you get through your rough time. In the end, you will be stronger and wiser. More importantly, your mess will become a message for someone else. Remember, your test is your testimony.

*God needs your mess to become a message for someone else.*

I'm writing this book because I believe deep, deep down inside that God has something bigger for all of the rejected stones of this world. Before you read any further or do anything else, I want you to find the window nearest you, look into the horizon, and say, "Today is a beautiful day."

# Chapter 2

# Inheritance from Godly (or Ungodly) Parents

*You raise me up, so I can stand on mountains;*
*You raise me up, to walk on stormy seas . . .*
—"You Raise Me Up" written by
Rolf Løvland and Brendan Graham

I was born the first time at Freedmen's Hospital in Washington, DC. I died and was reborn in a county jail in Las Vegas in 2007. My mother was with me at both of my birth places, which is pretty powerful to me. I was obviously too little to know the depth of my mother's love for me on my first birthday, but I learned all about the depth and breadth of Ma's unconditional love when she came with me to be fingerprinted and have a mug shot taken.

God doesn't make mistakes in selecting our parents.

My mother is a retired elementary school principal. She was in the first group of teachers who desegregated the Richmond, Virginia public schools after a federal judge ordered Richmond to obey the law and the US Constitution. My late father was a PhD scientist and was among the first graduating class of black students to ever receive a doctorate in zoology in 1963, the year of my birth. My stepfather was the recipient of the Purple Heart and Bronze Star and served in the US Army for thirty years, a Command Sergeant Major, a dog-faced soldier of the Third Infantry Division (Rock of the Marne!). There is no mistake that these individuals, each with distinct personalities and interests, were supposed to be in my life to help mold me into the person I am today.

*Not everyone is blessed with "good" parents, but I wouldn't call that a mistake either.*

Not everyone is blessed with "good" parents, but I wouldn't call that a mistake either. One of my law school classmates had such a chaotic childhood that she petitioned the court, as a teenager, to become emancipated. She even adopted her little brother, when she became twenty-one and he was seven, to get him out of the same chaos. Another one of my law school classmates, today a mother of ten (six when we were in law school together), had been tortured by her father as a child. Yes, that was my *same* reaction when I heard it, "Say what?!" One of her little brothers had actually been caged. The story was so off-the-chain crazy that I actually looked that case up myself. Today my friend's dad lives in a California penitentiary, and her mother would have also been there if she had not cut a deal with prosecutors and testified against her husband, who was the children's father. To add insult to injury, there are relatives who still accuse my friend and her brother of lying about what transpired.

Although God gave myself and each of my friends very different childhood experiences, we all ended up at the same intersection—law school. All three of us were selected as student attorneys at the Center for Legal and Social Justice at *St. Mary's Law School*, representing clients who could not afford lawyers. We were all vigorous student attorneys, especially when it came to dealing with families and children. We were fierce even before we were licensed. The point I'm attempting to make is that the inheritance that each of us received from our parents, whether it was good or traumatic, brought us all to the same place of grace.

Throughout my walk in the valley, during one of the darkest times in my life, I read Psalm 37. I read it at first because it was reaffirming that we should not worry about our enemies, but what I find awesome about reading the Word of God is that different things start to reveal themselves to you when you seek out God's message.

As I read Psalm 37, I started learning more about the true inheritance rights I personally had received from my parents. In verse 25, King David writes that he was once young but is now old, and in all that span of time, he had "never seen the godly abandoned or their children begging for bread" (NLT). When I went through my Las Vegas ordeal, I lost every penny to my name. Just an allegation of a wrongdoing in the public eye is enough to bankrupt anyone. Until your name is cleared, you can't really make a living because you are a social pariah, an outcast. For twenty months, I had no means of earning income. Although I received unemployment benefits, it covered only a fraction of my expenses. My savings were depleted, retirement accounts were gone, and I had to sell a good portion of my belongings on eBay and Craigslist. I had no financial resources, and I knew that if I were to walk into a welfare office, someone would

*I lost every penny to my name.*

tip off the Las Vegas media and they'd put it on the front page of the news. There was absolutely no reason I shouldn't have gone homeless and hungry, but Jehovah Jireh, my provider, showed up and explained to me why.

You see, I was an heir of godly parents. Not religious, Bible-thumping parents, but godly parents. I was the child of the type of people David wrote of in verse 25 of Psalm 37. The righteousness of my parents shielded me from all types of harm that should have come my way. I was compelled to start reading more about David himself. He was a flawed man, but he loved God, and God truly loved him. I mean, David committed adultery and had the woman's husband killed, but David acknowledged his shortcomings to God, and God really, really, really loved him deeply. As I read through the Bible about David's descendants in the book of Kings, from King Solomon and beyond, I started to notice a trend. David's descendants, including Solomon, would often get sideways with God. It seems the thing that really insulted God the most was that they would start worshiping other gods and idols. This always enraged God, but because of the covenant God made to David, their father, grandfather, great-great grandfather, etc., God spared the descendants even when He wanted to condemn them. David's relationship with God was their shield.

I started reflecting back on stories people would tell of my mother as a teenager. They told about her rounding up and picking up neighborhood kids and taking them to church. I reflected on how my late father, although a professor and dean, taught us how to always acknowledge the janitors in a college classroom building or library and to always thank them. When visiting my dad during the summers, I'd witness this simple act of kindness over and over again. My dad was a kind soul. I reflected on how my stepfather, although a senior himself, took care of his older sister with Alzheimer's who lived until she was ninety-three. When she finally had to be placed in assisted living, Sergeant Major (My name for him because he was a Command Sergeant Major in the US Army) visited her every single day without fail. It was quite a revelation, and humbling, for me to acknowledge that I probably was spared from begging for bread because of the favor my parents had earned from God. It had to do with *their* righteousness, not mine.

During that time, God brought Gordon and Carole Long into my life, a couple who attended the church I joined in 2006. That church was the International Church of Las Vegas (ICLV), pastored by Paul and Denise Goulet. My parents were in Texas and doing their best to lend their support across the miles, but I did not have them with me. Gordon and Carole stood in the gap for them. Not only did the Long's become like parents for me, they became the hands, arms, legs, and heart of Jesus to me.

Gordon and Carole were volunteers at a food pantry for needy families. Without asking them or even mentioning that I was in need, they took it upon themselves to pack up a box full of groceries for me and my children every Monday. After about two weeks of deliveries, I told them that they didn't need to drive to my house, that I would drive to the food pantry myself and gather groceries. They wouldn't let me do it. They insisted on bringing the food to me. This went on for close to a year. They also refused to let me go to court alone. They were always there, standing as parents, for me.

I moved to Texas in 2008, and Gordon Long passed away in 2010. Although I was unable to fly back to attend the funeral, I took time to write an account of what the Longs did for me. I have no doubt that Gordon is in heaven, and I wanted those in attendance to know publicly what they as a couple privately did for me.

My son was in middle school when all of this was happening. He is now a college freshman standing more than six feet tall. A few summers ago, we were in a grocery store in San Antonio just days before I was to sit for the Texas Bar Exam. The lady in front of us in the checkout line was short on cash. I could tell she was embarrassed that she was holding up the line and was frantically trying to figure out which groceries to take out of her cart. In that instant, I remembered Gordon and Carole, and I took cash from my wallet and paid the woman's balance. She was shocked and said, "Are you serious?"

I smiled and told her I was.

She asked what my name was, and when I told her, she said, "Lynette, I'll be praying for you."

When we got back to my apartment, I asked my son if he remembered how Gordon and Carole used to always bring us groceries.

"Oh, yeah, I do remember that!" he said.

I just took a few moments to share with him about God's covenant with David. As a mother of two, I now needed to live righteously myself so that my own children were never begging for bread. I have to form my own covenant with God, just like David did. As I benefited from my parents' relationship with God, my children will benefit from mine.

God made no mistake with the parents He sent you. He also has a way of sending stand-in-the-gap parents to

*God made no mistake with the parents He sent you.*

your life. I mastered the game face in public, but in private I could cry in Carole Long's arms. I knew I was loved and that it would be OKAY. Jesus showed up at my house with groceries every Monday for more than a year. Jesus held me and dried my tears. I was never forsaken. My children and I were never hungry.

A few people have said to me that it's been easier for me to have a good relationship with my parents and honor them because they were "good." In light of this, I started reflecting on people I know who, for a fact, didn't have good parents, as the world defines them. Many have nonetheless found a place of grace to have peace with those "bad" people who brought them into this world.

The Bible doesn't put a qualifier on honoring our parents. It doesn't say you should honor your parents only if you were fortunate to have good ones. The commandment is to honor your parents. One of my friends had a mother who would dress her up as an adult when she was twelve and thirteen and take her into bars to pick up men and bring them back to the house. My friend says it was but for the grace of God that she was never raped as a preteen. Through developing a personal relationship with God, my friend, now a grown woman, is able to see that her mother had serious mental health issues. My friend still remembers the past, but she has released it. She doesn't dwell there, and in her walk of faith, she has learned the power of forgiveness.

I would say the only method of being able to honor a parent under those type of circumstances must involve a heavy dose of forgiveness. If not, that "bad" parent will forever control your emotions—even when they're dead. It requires the Power/Love model taught at Gateway Church seminars. As Gateway teaches, we operate in either a Blame/Control or Power/Love mode. To dishonor a parent is operating in Blame/Control or "I'm not OKAY, and it's <u>all</u> your fault." Honor requires Power/Love: "I choose how I react to your actions. I control my happiness. I choose to love."

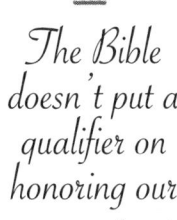

*The Bible doesn't put a qualifier on honoring our parents.*

৵৵

What is your relationship with your parents like? If you were to assess it honestly, are you in the Power/Love mode or the Blame/Control mode? No matter what they did to you—whether they abused, ignored, or abandoned you—the Bible says you must honor them. This requires a huge leap toward forgiveness. God cannot forgive us of our transgressions if we do not forgive those who have transgressed against us. It may require a great deal of prayer to get to the point where you can accept your parents' shortcomings in raising you. However, letting it go will lift a heavy burden from your heart—a burden you may have been carrying around for years or even decades—and give you peace, finally and forever.

When I see Facebook posts of individuals who haven't spoken to their parents in many years, I see the Blame/Control mode. The Bible teaches that this honor God asks isn't for our parents' benefit, but for our benefit. It is asked of children so that all will go well with *us*, not them. My friends who had "bad" parents but who choose Power/Love are the people who make everyone who comes into their company feel good and valuable. Ironically, that includes their parents. It may not look like honor the way the world describes it, but it is the honor that God requires when it comes to our parents, both the godly and the ungodly ones. If you can't see it today, it sounds to me like a start of your next prayer.

# Chapter 3

# Tree of Forgetfulness

*I returned for my children*
*I returned for my parents*
*I returned for the ones who went before*
*America to Africa once seemed so far away*
*Until today*
*He brought me back*
*I returned.*

—"I Returned" by Lynette Boggs Quintanilla

I was introduced to the person I consider my best male friend, Adam Rhodes, through one of my Miss Oregon sisters, Brook Roberts, who was Miss Oregon 2004. If her name sounds familiar, it's because you may have seen her in *The Amazing Race 17* or as a host on the Home Shopping Network. At the time, Adam and Brook were dating, and we all got to know each other at the 2006 Miss America Pageant, held in Las Vegas for the first time. Although Adam and Brook later parted ways, I will always be grateful to Brook for introducing me to one of the most rock-solid friends I've had in the past eight years.

Adam and I have never had any kind of romantic relationship. It's always been more like we were brother and sister growing up together, but for us, it was growing up together in our faith. Adam made and loss his fortune as a commercial real estate developer in Las Vegas. We met when we were both on top of our respective games— Adam through real estate, me through politics. Sharing a common desire to grow our faith and win souls for Christ, we decided to start a nonprofit together that we called FaithWorks Foundation. Our mission was rooted in James 2:18: "But someone will say, 'You have faith, and I have works.' Show me your faith without your works, and I will show you my faith by my works" (ESV).

We also formed a few small divisions within the framework of FaithWorks Foundation. We started a record label, 2:18 Records, and an internet radio station, 2:18 Radio. We were able to produce one album on our record label with Christian rapper, Chris LaVar. We also had several radio shows air original programming over the internet. I hosted my own weekly call-in radio show called *Restore*. One of my friends, Michelle Roberts, hosted a show aimed at getting women out of prostitution. Michelle's show was appropriately called *The Game*. There was also a show about male–female relationships hosted by Dr. William and Dr. Linda

Dougan. For several weeks, until conflicting schedules made it too difficult to continue, we also had *20-Something*, a show hosted by my friends, Christa Pitcairn and Lauren Goodman.

Once Adam and I had formally established FaithWorks Foundation, we invited two friends to serve on our board of directors: Arizona businessman Greg Francis, and former NBA player John Block. I had met both through Adam and knew immediately that they should advise us and help us develop our foundation's mission and direction. John had started his own successful community program in San Diego, called Lord's Fitness Center, which provided nutritional, educational, and athletic programs for inner-city children.

Every few years, John would make a mission trip to Ghana and Benin. He would deliver soccer balls to orphans in both of those countries and help spread the Gospel. During several of his visits to our FaithWorks offices, John, who happens to be white, would mention that it was critically important to him that if an African American ever joined him on the mission trip, he or she should be taken to Ouidah, one of the most prolific ports at the height of the transatlantic slave trade. During the seventeenth and eighteenth centuries and into the nineteenth century, it is estimated more than one million Africans were sold into slavery to the British, French, Portuguese, and Dutch at Ouidah. John felt strongly that I should visit Ouidah. My mother had previously visited slave ports in Ghana, but Ouidah was considered a slave port unlike any other. Something inside of me felt I needed to go there, so I told John I would very much like to accompany him on his mission trip so that I could see this place for myself. What had stirred up my strong desire to go was an experience that had happened to me at a Sunday evening service at ICLV. Pastor Paul had an altar call at the end of the service for anyone who had experienced generational curses in their family.

*More than one million Africans were sold into slavery to the British, French, Portuguese, and Dutch at Ouidah.*

When I first heard the call, my initial reaction was that it was for people who had come from families with alcoholism or possibly domestic violence, but I got convicted by the Holy Spirit as people were making their way up to the altar. I could hear the Spirit saying, "You've got a generational curse in your family, too." My generational curse was that of broken families.

I guess I had never really thought of it before, but almost no one in my family tree had grown up with their biological mother and father. My mother had, but when she was thirty, her father, on his deathbed, confessed that he had fathered a child with another woman. My grandmother, who died when my mother was twenty-six, never knew, to my mother's knowledge. Even my mother's immediate family had brokenness. My maternal grandmother's father had been killed when she was very young. Her mother, my great-grandmother, remarried but didn't want her daughter raised by a stepfather, so my grandmother was raised by her Aunt Maggie, her mother's sister. On my maternal grandfather's side of the family, my grandfather's father bore the last name Anderson, but Anderson was not his biological father. His biological father was a white Irish plantation owner in Athens, Georgia.

My parents divorced when I was about eight years old, and my father died in 1997. My father told me often of the story about how his own father, his namesake, abandoned the family during the Great Depression. My father grew up in Anniston, Alabama. He would often tell us about getting his haircut for his high school graduation at the neighborhood barber shop. The barber asked my father, then seventeen, if he knew who was sitting in the next chair. My father responded that he didn't. The barber told him, "That's your father, Nathaniel Boggs." My father said the man in the chair next to him had a monogram ring with the initials "N. B." My father said he recognized that, perhaps, the barber might be right, but he didn't know that man.

Of the four Boggs children, two of us have been divorced, and one of my brothers was a widower before he was forty. There have been a lot of broken families even in my own generation, so at that altar call, it was my prayer that if there was a generational curse in my family it would come to an end. I would stand in the gap for my entire family. The prayers were powerful that night at ICLV. I knew I wouldn't feel fully satisfied until I went back to the spot where that broken family curse all began—I had to go to West Africa.

*I wouldn't feel fully satisfied until I went back to the spot where that broken family curse all began—I had to go to West Africa.*

In June 2007, I joined John Block and Greg Francis on a mission trip to Ghana and Benin. We were joined in Accra by Missionary Ron Weeks who served as our translator in French-speaking regions such as Benin. We spent several days in Ghana and then began the trek through Togo, literally walking across the border into Benin. It was during the second or third day in Porto-Novo, the capital of Benin, when we were finally able to visit the shores of Ouidah.

The modern-day tour, Route of the Slaves, actually begins at a Portuguese fort. All of the other slave-trading nations had similar forts for hundreds of years, but only the Portuguese fort remains standing today. During the tour of the actual fort, now a historical museum, I was struck by the story of slave trade told to me by our Beninese tour guide. It was unlike anything that had been taught to me in American history class. For example, the tour guide emphasized how African chiefs and tribal leaders were in covenant with the slave traders. It was negotiated, and they had a pact to sell their own people. The tour guide also emphasized how families were split up. One family member would be put on a Portuguese ship, another would board a British Ship, and another a French ship. The tour guide told me that as an American, I probably had blood relatives in places like Brazil, Portugal, Great Britain, Guyana, Haiti, Cuba, and Holland, as well as throughout the United States.

I was taught throughout the tour about how the slaves were rounded up and put in total darkness to disorient them. Other hardships that were put upon them to get them ready for the voyage were explained. I saw some of the holding cells where hundreds upon hundreds were held before being marched out to the ships. This was those who had actually survived, as many never lived to board a ship.

John, Greg, Ron, the other missionaries, and I began walking toward the Atlantic Ocean along the Route of the Slaves. On the route was a monument to the Tree of Forgetfulness. Where there stands a monument today, there once stood a tree called the Tree of Forgetfulness. Before slaves would board the ships, the women would be required to walk around the tree seven times and the men nine times in a ritualistic fashion. According to the tour guide, as they marched around the Tree of Forgetfulness, a three-part voodoo curse was put on those in captivity. The three part curse was as follows:

1. That you would forget your identity
2. That you would forget where you came from
3. That you would never return

The purpose of the curse, according to our tour guide, was to ensure that no one would seek revenge on the chiefs and elders who had sold them to the slave traders.

After praying at the Tree of Forgetfulness monument, we finally made it to the Atlantic. I really can't put the experience into words, but a travail came over me on the shores of the Atlantic at Ouidah, and I wept so loud and so hard that everyone with me broke down and cried also. I guess it was the realization that a member of my family had endured one of the greatest atrocities of the human race. Just to get to the ship required survival. Making it to America was a miracle. For me, it was a recognition of gratefulness to all the generations of sacrifice that had gone before me. It was a travail of trust that I would never again deal with brokenness in my own life. It was a moment of hope that I was canceling the curse so that brokenness would not touch my children ever again, through me, or in their own future relationships. It was a travail that of my mother's

*A three-part voodoo curse was put on those in captivity.*

children, God would ordain it would be me to return and stand before the tree where a curse had been placed on my ancestors. It was a travail for all African Americans, especially African American men. The curse was bad enough for the women, but a greater curse was put on the men. Some may point to the election of President Barack Obama as proof that that black men can achieve if they just "buck up," but the ancestors of President Obama were never slaves. There was no marching around a tree

*A member of my family had endured one of the greatest atrocities of the human race.*

and receiving a curse on his lineage. All of these emotions and realities hit me all at once like a freight train's full impact.

I've never had struggle like that before, nor have I since. I went back to my hotel and cried for several more hours. The experience rocked me so much that I was compelled to channel my emotions into the writing of a song, "I Returned." I had never written music before, but in my hotel room that night in Porto-Novo, I wrote a song. I also accepted and acknowledged, for the first time, that I was a descendant of survivors, of overcomers, and that there would never be a situation or a person I would allow to break me. I had returned to Africa to honor my ancestors. It was then time to return to America, where a law enforcement was waiting to put chains on me. The devil himself was going to take me on to break me, my career, and my spirit. I was in for the fight of my life.

Whether it's a generational curse, a curse inflicted on one person by another or on one class of people by another, or a curse whose origin we cannot pinpoint, Satan is responsible, and God is the only one who can free one from it. If you were to look at your life as far back as you can, as many generations as you can, what do you see? What did your ancestors endure that carries over into your generation today? The source of your struggles may go back further than you might think, but healing can begin with you. If you are in the fight of your life, devote every bit of courage and faith that is within you to end the curse for good.

*What did your ancestors endure that carries over into your generation today?*

We all have God on our side to help us win the battles and the war.

# Chapter 4

# Betrayed with a Kiss

*Sometimes love can break your heart, but I'll die believing love is always worth the pain. Dreams may die or fall apart, but love's never given in vain.*
—"Sometimes Love Can Break Your Heart,"
written by Joel Lindsey
and recorded by Rick Brummett

To me, the ultimate betrayal is from someone who is close to you, knows you well, and then uses that knowledge to harm you. Many of the soldiers and temple police had never seen Jesus before, so on the night that Judas betrayed Jesus, Judas devised a special signal to alert them to who Jesus was so that they could capture and arrest him. Some Bible scholars refer to this type of betrayal from a trusted friend a "Judas kiss."

It is extremely difficult to forgive a betrayal from someone close to you. One of the hardest lessons I learned during my God chase was the lesson of forgiveness. I think most of us, on our own, can forgive the small stuff. It may indeed bother you, for example, when you loan money to a friend or relative and don't get it back. In time, most of us get over that kind of betrayal on our own though. I know I have.

The issue I dealt with—one that many of us have dealt with or will deal with if we live long enough—was a *big*-time betrayal. What I learned is that you can't get over these situations and move on alone. Only God can get you to that place of peace. Without God in the mix, the betrayer will likely continue to have control over your emotions, even when he or she is buried six feet under. It is only through a release of that betrayal to God that you can have forgiveness and peace that surpasses all understanding.

*The ultimate betrayal is from someone who is close to you, knows you well, and then uses that knowledge to harm you.*

I will never in my earthly, intellectual, tree-of-knowledge mind be able to wrap my head around why my former spouse testified against me before a grand jury. As a law school graduate, he certainly knew that the government could not compel him to testify due to spousal privilege. He also understood both the nature and consequences of the worst-case scenario—that I could be sent to prison and potentially be separated from my children for decades. On the day he testified, my parents, myself, and my high school friend, Mirna Packer, a pastor, all witnessed my ex-husband leave the courthouse. I can say it was one of the few times a situation caused me to be so physically nauseated that I almost threw up. I just never knew the depth of hatred a person could have toward me until that day. The experience brought me to a new awareness. I realized you can know me and hate me.

The testimony my ex-husband gave that day contributed to my indictment on four felony counts. My epitaph was written by several columnists in Las Vegas newspapers. Before O. J. Simpson knocked me off the front page for committing a robbery at the Palace Station hotel to get his sports memorabilia back, I was the most reviled person in Las Vegas.

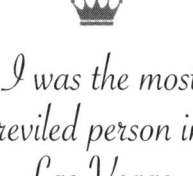

*I was the most reviled person in Las Vegas.*

Despite this fact, God was in control. Even as I felt my life spinning downward, and fast, God knew who needed to be in my life during that season, and he sent both the Goulets and the pastors of ICLV to me. Paul Goulet is the senior pastor of ICLV and, his wife, Denise, is a powerful pastor, as well, who preaches often at services. Although technology has given us the ability to read our Bibles from our phones, iPads, and tablets, I still typically use the Maxwell Leadership Bible that Paul and Denise gave me on the day, ironically, that I was sworn in as a Clark County commissioner.

There was a women's conference at ICLV around the time of all of this drama in my life, and a preacher from England, Rachel Hixson, was to deliver a message on forgiveness. The message and what happened after that message forever changed my life.

Rachel Hixson preached about Judas's betrayal of Jesus. Judas had been a trusted friend and was in Jesus' inner circle throughout His ministry, but he sold Jesus out for thirty pieces of silver. It was pretty low what Judas did, and although Jesus knew what had happened, he never condemned him. He only told him to do what he had to do.

What happened to Jesus from that point on can only be described as cruel and torturous. He was whipped, forced to carry a cross, and then nailed to that cross while being mocked the whole time. Rachel Hixson preached that day on the fact that Jesus never accepted bitterness. While hanging in agony on the cross, Roman soldiers attempted to put bitter wine on a sponge for him, but Jesus refused it. Even more amazing was the statement Jesus made before He commended His soul back to His Father. One of the last phrases He uttered before His death was "Father, forgive them, for they know not what they do" (Luke 23:34, ESV). Jesus was *only* about forgiveness, and that was the gist of the message Rachel Hixson preached.

After that message, I was standing near the altar in the

front of the ICLV sanctuary when Denise Goulet approached me and looked me in the eye. She said, "You know that message was for you." She didn't pose it as a question, she stated it as a fact.

She then sat me down on the steps of the altar and continued Rachel Hixson's message in a personal, made-just-for-me way.

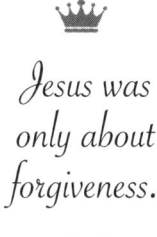

*Jesus was only about forgiveness.*

ॐ

She said I had to make a choice. Would I choose God's why or my way? Would I be bitter about the betrayals and all the things that had been going on in my life, or would I be better? She reminded me that what awaits on the other side of forgiveness is the most powerful gift of all—resurrection.

Now, I'm not going to lie to you. At that time I heard this message and had this conversation with Denise, I couldn't see how I'd ever be able to forgive or move past the trials I was experiencing. There was a period of time when it seemed I would notice every billboard for a gun show. I had never noticed them before, but I believe Satan was tempting me to take the easy way out and commit suicide. It was as if Satan was saying to me, "What do you have to lose? Why let the DA send you to jail?" I honestly believe, today, that Satan was going all out to turn me to evil, but there was something inside of me, something hard for me to even explain, that was much stronger than Satan's beckoning. The Holy Spirit was buried deep within me. It would not be extinguished. Like an eternal flame, it keep stirring in my subconscious mind. Deep, deep, deep inside, I knew that Pastor Denise was right about forgiveness.

But how would I get to that destination without a road map? I had to contend for it. As a little girl, I lived in Vicenza, Italy, for a year. My mother and stepfather also lived in Italy for a decade when I was an adult. My ex-husband and I had spent our honeymoon in Italy. In Italian, the word "contend" is *contendere*. In Italian, the word is used to describe a relentlessness toward something, to fight for something, to persevere through something. That's what I felt I had to do to find a place of forgiveness. I did it for the sake of my children, especially.

It required me to trust God like never before, but stories in the Bible helped me understand the concept and what I should do. After the story of Christ himself, the story of Joseph probably helped me the most. Joseph was sold into slavery by his own brothers. You could say he was also betrayed with a kiss, like Jesus was. Joseph's brothers were jealous of him, but he trusted them and didn't even realize he was about to be betrayed by those whom he loved so deeply.

In Egypt, Joseph was falsely accused and sent to prison, but he had a gift of interpreting dreams and he interpreted the dreams of fellow prisoners. Ultimately, his interpretation of Pharaoh's dream not only led to his release from prison, but to being elevated to the position of governor of Egypt. The only person more powerful than Joseph, in arguably the most powerful nation on the earth at that time, was Pharaoh himself.

As fate would have it, the very brothers who had sold Joseph into slavery ended up at his mercy. Joseph could have easily had his brothers put in prison at that point because the tables had been turned, but he didn't. He blessed them. Joseph's words to his brothers are so powerful to me, "You intended to harm me, but God intended it for good to accomplish what is now being done, the saving of many lives" (Genesis 50:20, NIV).

He blessed those who had cursed him. Joseph hugged his brothers. He ensured that they and their families would be provided for. In my own way, I knew I had to bless, not curse, my ex-husband.

I'm not a governor of a powerful nation, but I can still bless even in small ways. I can send a Father's Day card or a Happy Birthday text message. I can sit with my former spouse at school programs and pose for pictures so that my children need not have two sets of graduation pictures. I can give a hug. To do that was counterintuitive for the longest time. The natural tendency, our flesh way, is to do the exact opposite.

The image of my ex leaving the courthouse is forever burned in my mind, but it no longer causes the anger, anxiety, or nightmares of seven summers ago. It's only a memory now; it has no power over my emotions or peace of mind. For through the *contendere*, the persevering, I found forgiveness and peace. Most importantly, I don't need to try to figure out the question I was first plagued to ask, "Why did he do it?"

My ex remarried in October 2013. A friend contacted me privately on Facebook to see how I was holding up. Frankly, it was the oddest question to me because I was emotionally removed from the past at that point. It was a million light years away by 2013. I was full and have been living—and continue to—in a place of peace that surpasses my understanding. When she asked me, I shared with her and others on Facebook how Pastor Denise had challenged me to be "bitter or better." I explained how I had pressed toward an unknown mark. Although I found the message odd, it provided me with a checkpoint of where I was in my journey to forgiveness. As I told that friend and others, the only sentiment I had toward my ex was one of blessings. I sincerely wished him happiness.

*The image of my ex leaving the courthouse is only a memory now–it has no power over my emotions or peace of mind.*

My current pastor, Duane Lowe of New Life Fellowship in San Antonio, recently said something on this topic of forgiveness that really resonated with me. He reminded our congregation that when Jesus was on the cross, He said, "Father, forgive them, for they know not what they do" (Luke 23:34, ESV). They didn't know what they were doing to Jesus. They didn't get the big picture. Those hurting Jesus had a different context of what was going down. What causes us problems, Pastor Lowe reminded us, was that we assume the person harming us *does* know what he or she is doing. People might know at some micro level, but often their context of the situation and our context of the situation are not the same. They know *not* what they are doing. If we can get our heads around this concept and come to terms with it, I think it's so much easier to release what is holding us back from forgiving the person or situations that have caused us harm. Forgive them; they don't know what they're doing.

Jesus suffered one of the worst deaths imaginable. Our suffering is real, but it does not surpass what he endured. What have you suffered in your life that you have been unable let go of? Who in your past has caused you pain and heartbreak? Who has "betrayed you with a kiss"? Picture Jesus beside you. Remember how He suffered on the cross but still asked His Father to forgive them, for they know not what they do. With Jesus as your guide, make it your

*Let it go, once and for all. You will be "better" instead of "bitter".*

goal to let it go, once and for all. You will be "better" instead of "bitter" as a result, and that will only enrich your life from this moment on.

# Chapter 5

# The Three Davids

*When the spirit of the Lord comes upon my heart,*
*I will dance like David danced.*
*I will dance. I will dance. Dance, like David danced.*
—Popular Song, Unknown Author

While attending a Sunday morning class at a church in San Antonio, the teacher introduced me to a book titled *A Tale of Three Kings* by Gene Edwards. It was a story about Saul, David, and Absalom and covered the leadership styles of these three rulers of Israel. I think most people know about David. After all, he wrote so many of the Psalms and was a man after God's own heart. It was not until I read *A Tale of Three Kings* and reflected on these three rulers; however, that something dawned on me. The men who probably had the most to do with my spiritual death and rebirth were all named David. They were David Roger, David Kallas, and David Groover.

Other than to write this chapter, I really haven't thought about these men often. David Roger was the District Attorney of Clark County. David Kallas was the head of the Las Vegas police union. And David Groover was the private investigator who put my children and me under surveillance so that they could prove I didn't live where I said I lived. In the short term, these three men prevailed. In the long term, I've prevailed.

If there's anything I could add to my case in Las Vegas, it is that I know for a fact that David Groover videotaped myself and my children at the house I allegedly never lived in. When I was first sued, but before I was charged criminally, David Groover personally served me at the front door of that house. When service of process documents are returned to the court, notifying the court that the person sued has received notice, those documents are supposed to list the specific address where the documents were served and to whom. David Groover left that section blank when he filed those documents with the Clark County District Clerk, and I'm fairly confident that he didn't share this information with the grand jury either. I can't envision a world in which David Kallas would not have knowledge of this omission to the court. After all, he used his 100 percent government-funded position as union president to direct the entire endeavor. If David Roger was aware of these facts, he would have been in violation of the Supreme Court holding in *Brady v. Maryland* because this evidence and the video footage of me at the other house was never shared with my defense counsel.

That said, it's pretty much a moot point today as far as I'm concerned. I'm a million miles removed from that whole season of my life. Ironically, I owe these Davids a lot. Because of them, I became a worshipper like the David of the Bible. The three Davids who were working against me gave me a triple anointing, but God has already turned the evil they attempted around for my good.

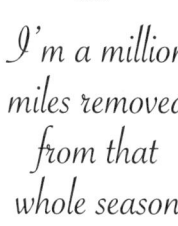

*I'm a million miles removed from that whole season in my life.*

It was at ICLV where I learned the freedom of worship. When I was a little girl in Virginia, I would either go to the African Methodist Episcopal (AME) church with my mother or to Catholic Mass with my father. I was raised Catholic because of my father, but at the AME church as a little girl, I saw women crying out or shouting, lifting their hands in praise, and sometimes jumping out of their seats. I didn't understand it at the time, but today, I do.

When King David was bringing the ark of God to the City of David, the Bible says that he danced before God in such a way that his wife got embarrassed about it. She even attempted to admonish him for dancing in public like that, but David didn't care what it looked like to those watching. I can only imagine what was running through David's mind at the time. He was probably just dancing in remembrance of *all* the things God had brought him through.

So many stories about the life of David have inspired me. I want to share with you a few of them, or at least the points that truly have stood out to me about David. The first is that he was the baby brother of Jesse's sons. No one expected him to be the chosen one, yet he was chosen. As a teenager, he was the one who had the courage to fight Goliath. His older brothers were already on the battlefield with Saul. David was only there to deliver rations, but he wasn't intimidated by Goliath because God had already delivered him from "lions and bears." As a kid, he was already aware of what God had brought him through and what God was capable of doing.

My second favorite story of David's life was when he sent his men to get supplies from a man named Nabal. David and his men had protected the lands of Nabal during war, so David didn't think it would be a problem to go to this man to get restocked on some items they needed for the battlefield. Surprisingly, Nabal copped an attitude and sent a message back to David basically saying he could care less about David or his needs. When this message got back to David, David's initial reaction was probably the reaction most of us would have when we've helped someone and then they pay us back with disrespect. David was going to take out Nabal's entire household. Fortunately, Nabal's wife, a woman named Abigail, heard about how her husband had disrespected the king. She gathered everything David had requested and took the supplies to him herself. Because of Abigail's actions, David had a change of heart and decided not to attack Nabal.

What I personally learned from this story is that I just need to ignore people who offend me. To play "tit for tat" or to seek revenge just isn't worth it. It is better to take the high road and move on. God will take care of your enemies. Going back to Nabal and David, when Nabal heard what his wife had done, he had a heart attack and died. In the end, Nabal died without David having to do anything. David then married Abigail, but that wasn't the part of the story that has stayed with me. They key point for me was recognizing that human nature and God's nature are not the same. David didn't need to do anything. God took care of his enemies, and He will take care of your enemies, too. It is not your place to do so. Call on

*To seek revenge just isn't worth it. It is better to take the high road and move on.*

God. He will orchestrate a plan that surpasses human understanding and takes care of the situation in a way you could never dream of.

I also love the story of David and Bathsheba. It illustrates how even someone greatly loved by God can mess up. David committed adultery and arranged for Bathsheba's husband to be killed so that he could have her as his own. Despite this moral error, David never lost his tie to God. He worshipped, even when God took the life of the first child born to David and Bathsheba. David worshipped.

God had brought David through so much through his life, so when the spirit of the Lord came upon David, like the women in that AME church, he felt compelled to dance. When he did, he danced with all his might, not caring what it looked like.

Today, my spirit feels trapped if I go into a church where praise and worship are considered strange or undignified. Strange was how Saul's daughter looked at it, and when she criticized David for his worship, God made it so that she would never give birth, ever. I have to attend a church where I can get my praise on. Breakthrough is in the praise. Deliverance is in the praise. Healing is in the praise. Praise confuses Satan because he can't understand why you're honoring God when your child just died, your car got repossessed, or you lost your job.

*I have to attend a church where I can get my praise on. Breakthrough is in the praise.*

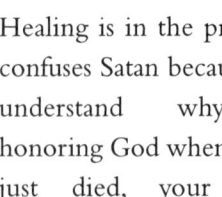

If you want to see a church that's growing, it's typically a house of worship where praise is encouraged. Where praise is stifled or discouraged, the church likely is in a slump, facing both financial and spiritual challenges.

My three Davids may have pursued me like Saul, but I inherited a triple anointing of praise for God. When His spirit comes upon me, these days, I can do only one thing and that is dance.

Who are the "three Davids" in your life? If you look closely enough, you will see that the thorny situations others may put you through can work out for good— some way, somehow. When someone does something to try to bring you down, your first response is probably to want revenge or to feel depressed, but that isn't where the lesson is. The lesson is buried deep within your pain. Look there to discover the seed of good that God has planted to mold you and shape you into a testament of His grace.

Once you find it, you, too, will want to dance.

# Chapter 6

# Jezebel

*So Jezebel sent this message to Elijah: "May the gods strike me and even kill me if by this time tomorrow I have not killed you just as you killed them." Elijah was afraid and fled for his life. He went to Beersheba, a town in Judah, and he left his servant there. Then he went on alone into the wilderness, traveling all day. He sat down under a solitary broom tree and prayed that he might die. "I have had enough, LORD," he said. "Take my life, for I am no better than my ancestors who have already died."*

— 1 Kings 19:2-4 NLT

For most of my life, I had heard the terms "the devil" and "evil," but I never fully appreciated what they meant. I remember the story in the Bible about Jesus being tempted in the desert and how He rebuked Satan, but for most of my life in the church, Satan was kind of like the Easter Bunny—almost a mythical figure. If he had a beef, it was with Jesus and God, and I really didn't have a dog in the fight—or so I thought.

I probably wasn't a threat to Satan by having this kind of mindset, but if there's something I learned in my God chase of the past seven years, it's that Satan is *real*. Satan doesn't have a large playbook because he's a defeated foe, but he can wreak havoc in your life. You may not even know you're actually under a spiritual attack when certain situations trigger a migraine headache or insomnia, but once you can recognize the limited playbook, you can equip yourself to deal with Satan and his minions who still roam the earth.

*You can equip yourself to deal with Satan and his minions who sill roam the earth.*

The three plays are found in John 10:10. As told by Jesus, "The thief comes only to *steal* and *kill* and *destroy*" (ESV). I attended a women's conference in March 2013 at ICLV. The main speaker was Christian author and teacher, Lisa Bevere. She said in one of her messages that the enemy's main objective is to "diminish you, distract you, and divide you." I'd add a few "A's" to that list, as I've found that Satan also aims to antagonize, annoy, and annihilate us.

Before I began my God chase, I used to just accept as gospel pretty much anything that was being preached from a pulpit. As I grew closer to God, I began to discern what was truly of God and what was from the enemy—even from people preaching from pulpits. I became a lot more in tune with whether or not to receive prophetic words that had been spoken over my life. As I got deeper into the reading of the Word of God, I began to accept that words of prophecy that are truly heaven-sent are for up building, encouragement, and consolation. If what a friend, a lover, an employer, or even your pastor is speaking to you leaves you beat down, discouraged, and feeling hopeless, consider it a wake-up call. The words you are hearing may not be coming from God but from some other place.

When I think about that story of Jesus and Satan, I've reflected a lot about some of the key scenes. What has stood out for me was that the enemy showed up when Jesus was alone and feeling physically weak. I have found in my own walk that one of the most effective schemes Satan can use is to keep us isolated from other people. Most of our societal ills, from suicide to pornography addiction, or eating disorders (binging or eating excessively), occur—or can occur more easily—when we're isolated from people. We see it in Matthew 4. Satan endeavored to tempt Jesus with food and with jumping off a cliff.

Have you ever noticed that when you felt weak, depressed, sick, or alone, was when Satan tempted you and tried to sway you from your walk with God? Pay attention during those times. Call on God to strengthen your spiritual resolve when you are feeling physically or emotionally defeated.

The enemy wanted to kill or diminish Jesus that day because even he knew the promise of what was in the future.

He wants to kill and diminish you for the same reasons.

One of the generals in Satan's army was Jezebel. She was the princess found in the Hebrew book of Kings, the daughter of Ethbaal, King of Tyre (Phoenicia) and the wife of Ahab, king of north Israel. I encourage you to read about her, but I'll cut to the chase. She had an agenda to kill prophets of God. The prophet Elijah so feared her that he ran into a cave to hide from her and save his life.

The Jezebel spirit is alive and well today. The purpose of this spirit is to cause you so much fear and trepidation

*The purpose of the Jezebel spirit is to cause you so much fear and trepidation that you run and hide.*

that you run and hide. This spirit works overtime to diminish you, to destroy you, and to isolate you from the ones who need to hear your voice the most.

A columnist in Las Vegas with the spirit of Jezebel used to attempt to run me into a cave, antagonize me, and diminish me. This individual has called me a liar so many times that my pants should have certainly caught on fire by now. Although I have not seen, spoken with, or returned a message to this individual in more than seven years, this columnist will still, from time to time, target me in a publication with the sole purpose of distracting and diminishing me. The Jezebel spirit, in the form of these writings, will attack the things I'm most sensitive about, especially reminding me of my failed marriage. These columns stir up all types of evil. I have received anonymous e-mails from individuals who have no problem calling me a "nigger," "cunt," "criminal," "bitch," and, of course, "liar."

But like Jesus, I rebuke that spirit because I recognize it for what it is. I will never say I haven't made big mistakes in my life. I have, but I refuse to be defined by them. My great-grandmother once told me, "It's not what they call you, it's what you answer to." I refuse to answer to anything that isn't of God. God says I'm blessed and highly favored, that I'm more than a conqueror, and that I'm the head and not the tail.

*It's not what they call you, it's what you answer to.*

The last attack I withstood took place on the day of the annual Fiesta Farewell that my law school gives to its graduating class. It was a day that should have been filled with celebration, but the Jezebel spirit caused my Samsung phone to blow up with hate e-mails. Some of the messages declared that I would *never* be allowed to become a lawyer because of the things I went through in Las Vegas. It would have been very easy to isolate myself and internalize all of the negativity, but I refused to because I recognized it for what it was—a spiritual attack.

I had a standing study session with my law classmate, Ling Han, so that we could review for an oil and gas class that both of us had taken to prepare us for the Texas bar examination. Ling could see that my phone was alerting me to e-mail after e-mail and that something was distracting me. In the law library in San Antonio, I told her about the column that had been written about me. Without hesitation, she had me log in to my e-mail account, and then she did something I didn't even know could be done. She created hate filters for my e-mail account so that if certain words ever appeared in an e-mail message to me, the message would be deleted immediately and I would never see it. In about three minutes, Ling Han shut the messages completely down. I was stunned. We even added other hateful words that I hadn't yet received. We started brainstorming and adding to the filters.

I could have easily isolated myself, but I didn't. Instead, I rebuked Satan. That day, God sent a classmate to minister to me by using her technology skills to give me peace. I could have easily been sitting in the library with my blessing sitting across from me and kept my mouth shut. What was happening could have easily pushed me into a depression. It could have easily filled me with self-doubt about becoming a lawyer right before it was time to study for my final exams and begin my studies for the bar exam. The Jezebel spirit was making a last-ditch effort to run me into a spiritual and psychological cave, but I didn't let that spirit win.

My closest friends will tell you that I listen to all genres of music, including country music. One of my favorite country artists of all time is the late Johnny Cash. I often reflect on his testimony of when he was shackled with addictions, depressed, and at the lowest point of his life. He went to Nickajack Cave on the Tennessee River, just north of Chattanooga, to end his life. Yes, a cave. Stories and articles have been written about Johnny Cash. They say it was in that cave where the singer said he had an encounter with God. Cash wrote about his experience. "There in Nickajack Cave, I became conscious of a very clear, simple idea: I was not in charge of my destiny. I was not in charge of my own death. I was going to die at God's time, not mine. I hadn't prayed over my decision to seek death in the cave, but that hadn't stopped God from intervening."

The story goes on that Johnny Cash literally crawled out of the cave. Prophets don't belong in caves. Even Elijah, whom Jezebel had run into hiding, came out. God Himself finally said to him, "What are you doing here, Elijah?" (1 Kings 19:9, ESV). The message is clear. Get out of the cave!

If there's something I've learned from the Jezebel spirit, it's that Jezebel only attacks out of fear. I'm not diminished, because God's promises are true. I am blessed and highly favored. I'm more than a conqueror; I'm

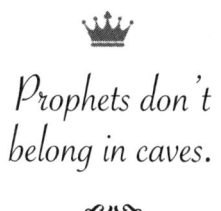

*Prophets don't belong in caves.*

the head and not the tail. And guess what? *You* are, too. If we are run into the cave, our voices and testimonies are silent. Our ability to build, encourage, and console others is lost. To that I say, the devil *is* a liar. I will not be run into a cave.

Is the Jezebel spirit trying to run you into a cave? Do you feel fear gripping you in a certain aspect of your life? Turn the fear over to God, and He will walk with you out of the cave, with your head held high and your heart full of peace. The spirit of Jezebel is no match for God's mercy.

By the way, Jezebel didn't have a good ending. She was eventually devoured alive by a pack of dogs. It's in the Bible.

# Chapter 7

## Ignatius

*Take, Lord, and receive all my liberty, my memory, my understanding and my entire will. All I have and call my own, You have given to me; to you, Lord, I return it. Everything is yours; do with it what you will. Give me only your love and your grace. That is enough for me.*

— *English translation of* Suscipe Domine *written by Ignatius of Loyola, founder of the Society of Jesus, a Christian male religious congregation of the Catholic Church. Its members, which include Pope Francis, are called Jesuits.*

Although I rarely worship in a Catholic church today, I have a great love for the Catholic Church because it has played a substantial role in the development of my faith and greatly influenced my career choice as a criminal defense lawyer. I am a graduate of both the *University of Notre Dame* in South Bend, Indiana, and of *St. Mary's University School of Law*, the sole

Catholic law school in the state of Texas. My paternal great-grandmother, Emma Cooper, was one of the first black people in Anniston, Alabama, to convert to Catholicism in the 1930s, and Mass was frequently held in her home until an actual church structure for All Saints Catholic Church was built for black Catholics in Anniston. My father's funeral was held at All Saints in 1997. At that time, I had received all of the Sacraments of the church, short of Last Rites. There are many Catholic priests, nuns, and bishops whom I count as friends and mentors, both then and now.

When I went through my desert season, I felt I needed to take my worship in another direction. I needed and desired to take my faith to a deeper level. For me, the Catholic Church was my comfort zone, but to grow and to be able to develop a personal relationship with God, I needed to find another faith experience. I needed to find a place where I could chase God only—nothing and no one else. Despite this, I was never very far from the Catholic Church, and my love for it remains strong to this day.

My second year of law school was extremely stressful. As is the common saying at most law schools, the first year they scare you to death, the second year they work you to death, and the third year they bore you to death. My second year was definitely my work-you-to-death year. During that time, I was invited to be a staff writer for Volume 42 of *St. Mary's Law Journal*. I represented St. Mary's both regionally and nationally in moot court competitions. I also was a student attorney at the Center for Legal and Social

Justice. Lest I forget, I also took fifteen hours of classes every semester, which required reading assignments and preparation for being called on in class every day.

When you get caught up in sixteen to eighteen hour days and experience sleep deprivation, it can become easy to get stressed out and overwhelmed. Additionally, during the second year many law students are trying extremely hard to secure a summer internship or clerkship. I was no exception. The thought behind this concept is that

*I needed to find a place where I could chase God only – nothing and no one else.*

gaining a clerkship allows a future employer to test-drive you while you're still a student, giving one a leg up on securing a "real lawyer" job with that employer after graduation.

I had become a finalist for two jobs in Washington, DC, for the summer between my second and third years. One was for a prestigious environmental law firm that would pay me $10,000 per month. The other was to work as a public defender for no pay. My heart wanted to be a public defender, but my head wanted me to be an environmental lawyer. This created an internal conflict because I had been broke, living month to month, hand to mouth, for several years at that point. On top of that, I was just plain exhausted from everything else going on in my academic life.

During that time, I was assigned to work as a student attorney on a case to help a family on the Texas–Mexico border who was about to lose their home due to foreclosure. My supervising attorney was Sister Susan Skidmore, a Catholic nun who is licensed as a lawyer in both Louisiana and Texas. Working with Sister Susan, I had many occasions to tell her about my children and of my desire to serve God through the practice of law. While updating Sister Susan on the foreclosure case, she must have sensed in her spirit that something was going on in my life. She asked me about it and I shared with her the internal conflict between following my heart and being a responsible adult and single mother. Shouldn't I just take the money and run? Can't I just use the one job to get me financially straight and then take the job I *really* want to do later?

Sister Susan said simply, "*Suscipe*." My initial reaction, of course, was that she was dropping some legal term. Noticing the look of confusion on my face, she said it again, "*Suscipe*, that Ignatius prayer." It dawned on me that what she was referencing was a prayer written by Ignatius Loyola, the theologian who founded of the Society of Jesus in 1541. We refer to this Order of priests as the Jesuits.

As a choir member of the St. James Gospel Choir when I attended a Catholic church in Las Vegas, I remembered singing a song called "Take, Lord, Receive." I knew the words to the song, but until Sister Susan had mentioned it, I never connected the dots between those lyrics and the prayer written by Ignatius of Loyola. Reading those words and later downloading a song by composer Paul Melley, I was rocked. In fact, I was so rocked by the words that I broke down and wept in the law library that evening when I took the time to reflect on what Sister Susan had been trying to communicate to me when she

*She said it again, "Suscipe, that Ignatius prayer."*

ॐॐ

told me of the *Suscipe* prayer. This has become my prayer of surrender, acceptance, and peace:

*Take, Lord, and receive all my liberty,*
*my memory, my understanding,*
*and my entire will,*
*All I have and call my own.*
*You have given all to me.*
*To you, Lord, I return it.*
*Everything is yours; do with it what you will.*
*Give me only your love and your grace,*
*that is enough for me.*

I realized that there were a whole lot of things in my life that I had been holding on to for so long, not even realizing it. It was finally time to return them to the One who gave them to me in the first place, God.

In the order of the prayer, I had to give up my liberty first. As a criminal defense lawyer, to lose one's liberty is pretty serious. To give up your liberty means you no longer have the right to call the shots anymore. You have to accept what you're told to do and do it. You no longer have the power; that power belongs to someone else. If you don't

*I had to give up my liberty first.*

surrender, a warrant will be issued for your arrest. You either surrender yourself or you will be found and forcibly taken into custody. To give up my liberty meant it wasn't going to be my call anymore where I was going to work. I was to accept the call

from God. I was to go where God was sending me, and I knew in my heart that God was sending me to serve the poor. Ultimately, I needed to go where my source, my higher power, was telling me to go.

Giving my memory back to God next was probably the most painful thing to do. There were things so painful that had happened in my past, that to recall them or even speak of them took many years. One day, I shared with my parents my experience of being shackled the day I was arraigned in Las Vegas. In the Clark County Detention Center, there is a device that is like a six-inch-wide leather belt that fastens behind you with handcuffs attached to the front. It's impossible to move your wrists away from your waist area once you're put into this device. I'm a slightly claustrophobic person, so the restraint made me start to have a slight anxiety attack. It was hard to breathe. After the death of my sister-in-law and niece in a tragic automobile accident in 2005, being placed in this restraint was probably the most traumatic personal experience I've ever endured. With the exception of one of my nephews, no one in my family had any familiarity with being a defendant in the criminal justice system, but it was in that place of desperation where God showed Himself strong to me. I died and was born again in that moment. I've never been the same since then.

I freely share that memory today, but when I shared it with my parents, even they were unaware of what an ordeal I had experienced and that I had never shared it with anyone before them. They cried with me, and then my dad prayed for healing for me. I later shared this experience with my nephew, who served time in a Nevada state prison. It made him cry when I told him, "We're the only ones who've had this experience in our family, so we're more alike than you might think." What was a painful memory gives me a heart of empathy for the clients I serve today. But for the grace of God, go I.

I've attended fine universities. When I received both my master's and doctor of jurisprudence degrees, I had honor cords around my neck. I think a challenge I face being a highly educated person, especially one who earns a living making arguments, is that I can overthink and overanalyze things. Adam and Eve also struggled with this need for understanding and knowledge that didn't belong to them. They had the Tree of Life, but got tempted to eat from the Tree of Knowledge because they thought it would give them the ability to know what God knows.

Going back to my dilemma of where to work after my second year of law school, as a single mom, I was asking the question, "How am I going to work for the public defender service in Washington, DC for free?" *Suscipe* taught me to stop trying to understand the "how" behind the things I knew were from God. I realized I had to give up my understanding.

Finally, I had to give back to God my entire will. Don't get me wrong, I struggle with surrendering all of the things in Ignatius of Loyola's prayer, but I think that giving my will to God may be the hardest of all. Even before I became a lawyer, I had a tendency to cut my losses when things got tough, especially in my romantic relationships. In criminal law, a "willful" mental state isn't a good one. In the courtroom, it means you have been deliberate and calculating in committing a particular crime. In life, even when you're attempting to do good, being deliberate and calculating in your goodness can be a bad thing. I learned the importance of surrendering my will, and to this day, it's a daily, sometimes hourly, effort.

*Suscipe* challenges you to give *everything* that has been given to you *back* to God so that He can use it as He wills. That meant I had to give my children back to God, my relationships with my parents and siblings back to God, my career and accomplishments back to God, and even my husband, Michael, back to God.

In return for my giving liberty, memory, understanding, will, and everything to God, I received freedom and peace coming from the realization that one truly needs only two things to make it in this life. They are love and grace. Ignatius realized that despite having only those two things, he was a rich man. I tell people all the time, "I was most miserable in my life when I lived in a five-thousand-square-foot house and had a lot of money in the bank." When I lost it all, I was stripped of everything, except love and grace. It was then that I became rich. That discovery was paradoxical for me. Don't get me wrong, I like depositing money in my bank account from my hard work in the practice of law, but that doesn't make me a rich person. I'm full,

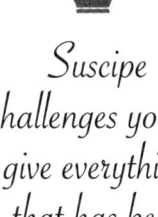

*Suscipe challenges you to give everything that has been given to you back to God so that He can use it as He wills.*

rich, and at peace because I'm filled with love and grace. That is enough for me.

Is it enough for you? When you think about giving back your liberty, power, memory, understanding, will, relationships, career, wealth, comfort, and everything else to God, which one is the most difficult for you? Why? Work on it. Make it your goal to give it all back to God. I assure you, He will return it all to you, and more. He will bless you with more gifts than you ever hoped for once He sees that you are obedient to His will and purpose.

# Chapter 8

# Ain't No Half-Steppin'

*Better is one day in your courts*
*than a thousand elsewhere;*
*I would rather be a doorkeeper in the house of my God*
*than dwell in the tents of the wicked.*
— Psalm 84:10 NIV

I think it's safe to say that most have heard the story of Moses bringing the Hebrews out of slavery in Egypt and about the parting of the Red Sea. We have heard of the Ten Commandments brought down by Moses from Mount Sinai, and probably know that Moses never made it to the Promised Land. That task was left to his assistant, Joshua.

One of my goals in writing this book is that people will seek out what God wants to tell them through His word. I can accomplish that only by sharing how God's promises found in these biblical stories have played out in my own life. Everything God promised Moses, He promised to Joshua, and everything He promised to Moses and Joshua, He also promises to every one of us. I'm not special; neither were Moses or Joshua, but they were available.

The concept I have grasped from the story of Joshua is that God truly will give you territory in every place you put your foot down. However, you're only going to have dominion if you can see the place you're standing through spiritual eyes.

*You're only going to have dominion if you can see the place you're standing through spiritual eyes.*

Over the course of eighteen months, beginning in 2006, I was sued civilly, I was charged criminally, and I went through a divorce. These situations caused me to file a Chapter 7 in US bankruptcy court because of the mountain of legal bills I had. Financially, I was wiped out. There was a period of time when I was literally in some type of court every day. At the time, I felt I was cursed. I was depressed, and thoughts of suicide ran through my head from time to time. I wondered how I could escape my misery.

Today, I know it was all strategic planning for the crossover God was setting me up for. I was not aware of what God was up to, but He was molding me into a trial lawyer. At the same time, He was removing scales from my eyes so that I could see as my future clients would see. By having me go through this, God was giving me a heart transplant. He was giving me empathy that I could not have achieved any other way.

The pieces started to come together for me during my second year at St. Mary's when I served as a student attorney at the Center for Legal and Social Justice. I feel fairly confident in saying I had more cases that were ultimately litigated than other students in that clinic. My first case involved a woman who had been denied Social Security benefits. When I first met her, I immediately noticed that we were born on the same day. It was as though God was sharing with me that it was through His grace that I was the attorney and this woman the client. The tables could have easily been turned.

The second case I litigated involved a young mother with two children. She wanted full custody of her children because her estranged husband was a meth user. The third case I litigated was representing a family on the Texas–Mexico border who had a home in foreclosure. During that year, I also handled real estate transactions, wrote wills, and helped victims of domestic violence obtain protective orders or get out of leases, but those three litigated cases were my big cases.

All of those courthouse appearances I had made in Las Vegas prepared me to feel at ease now in a courtroom. The environment was familiar to me. I had already observed how lawyers conducted themselves "inside the well." I saw the formalities. I knew at which table the defense sat. I knew where the court clerks sat and recorded the proceedings. I learned all of this as the defendant in both a divorce proceeding and a criminal proceeding. As a result, when I enter a courtroom today, I know God has given me dominion as a trial lawyer. My experiences, which were unpleasant at the time, were actually preparing me for a successful career as an attorney.

I was one of the students who competed in courtroom advocacy competitions in both moot court and mock trial. Representing my law school in both regional and national competitions, I was one of ten in my class inducted into the national Order of Barristers. The Faculty Advocacy Committee also presented me with its most prestigious annual advocacy award, the Judge Jack B. Miller Award.

In my first year as a Texas lawyer, I represented more than one hundred indigent children and adults charged with crimes in Bexar, Wilson, and Atascosa Counties. I had two jury trials and also assisted a seasoned criminal defense lawyer in a capital murder trial that ultimately ended in a plea (as most criminal cases do). I am also one of the appointed lawyers for the Texas Department of Pardons and Parole and have represented many inmates in revocation hearings.

I dreaded court appearances seven years ago. Today, it's a bad day if I'm not in court. There's a contemporary Christian worship song titled "Better Is One Day" that has been recorded by many artists, including Matt Redman and the rock group, Kutless. Its chorus recalls

Psalm 84:10, which states that one day in God's courts is better than a thousand elsewhere. I know this fact to be true. I'm living the reality of the song in a literal and spiritual way.

The point of this chapter is to cause you to pause and think about where your feet are right now. Where has God placed you? Is it a place of dread in your mind? Are you looking at it as a curse, as I once did? I challenge you, like God challenged Joshua, to look neither to the left nor to the right. Look straight ahead. This place of heartbreak, this place of disappointment, through spiritual eyes, just might be your training ground. Look at it differently. I believe God is giving you dominion in that very thing. Will you claim your territory?

*Look straight ahead. This place of heartbreak, this place of disappointment, through spiritual eyes, just might be your training ground.*

There is one more important thing that I'd like to mention on that note. God promised the children of Israel a pretty huge territory; however, the land they actually claimed was but a fraction of that which was promised. I once read that what was claimed by Israel represented only 10 percent of what was actually promised. As the book of Joshua states, God promised the following to the children of Israel: "Your territory will extend from the desert to Lebanon, and from the great river, the Euphrates—all the Hittite country—to the Mediterranean Sea in the west" (Joshua 1:4, NIV). This territory, even in 2015, has never been fully claimed.

What I've noticed in life and pulled from these stories during my God chase is that there are people who choose to camp and those who choose to cross over. Camping can be fun. I did it as a Girl Scout and with my family as a little girl. It was a place of campfires and s'mores then. For the children of Israel, camping involved building monuments and idols. They seemed to always see the glass as half empty when they were camping, and they were often complaining because of what they thought they were lacking.

Crossing requires another skill set. First and foremost, it requires faith. You don't know what lies ahead; you just know you have to move in that direction, no matter what. A crossing mentality requires that even from a place of lacking, you see what you have with a spirit of gratitude. Having a crossing mentality requires that you keep a setback in context of the overall, big-picture objective.

In my final year of law school, I signed up for all kinds of interviews with law firms and government agencies. I would always get invited back for second interviews, but I was never offered an associate's position. Our career services dean would often tell our graduating class to "think outside the box" with our job search because our entire country was in a recession, and it was likely that very few of us were going to be hired. She said that even in Texas, we'd be competing against Harvard and Yale law grads who happened to be from Texas, not to mention Baylor and University of Texas law grads. If I had a camp-out mentality, I could have spent months sending out hundreds more résumés to no avail. I could have gotten frustrated about having spent more than a hundred grand for a legal education and not finding a legal job to help me pay off the debt.

I decided to cross over instead, by charting unknown territory. I hung out a shingle and started my own law practice. Now, I doubt I'll ever work for anyone but myself again. Every day I ask God to help me to claim 100 percent of the promises He has spoken over my life. I claim every promise of Moses and Joshua as my own. Looking neither to my left nor my right, I'm claiming as my territory every place my foot touches. We can be saved and still not achieve the full promise. It requires pressing, and it requires a crossing mentality. Ten percent is not acceptable. I want 100 percent of all God has promised me in this life.

You probably know some people who camp and others who tend to cross over when they are confronted by setbacks. We tend not to respect or enjoy

*Look neither to my left nor to my right, I'm claiming as my territory every place my foot touches.*

the company of the campers. Crossing over requires strength, courage, faith, and fortitude. Be the one who crosses over. Be the one others look up to when a setback has everyone else on the precipice of a breakdown. Be the one standing tall and claiming territory for your walk with God. Refuse to let hardship or difficulty stand in the way of claiming the victory for your own future and for God's glory.

# Chapter 9

# Pride and Shame

*Well I'm going home,*
*Back to the place where I belong,*
*Where your love has always been enough for me.*
—"Home" by Chris Daughtry

Pride and shame are two powerful strongholds, and many of us can go through life not even realizing we're shackled by them. Our pride and shame prevent us from acknowledging our pride and shame, but these are real dangers and can prevent us from walking into the fullness of God's intended promise.

I made six figures for many years and lived a great material life. At one point, I defined success by the world's definition of success. That is, I lived in a big house, I wore designer clothes, I drove a Volvo, and my kids were in private school. I was living the dream—or so I thought.

When all of that came crashing down around me, I

was unable to feed my children or pay my bills. I had no income; I had no job. As I mentioned, I knew that, at least in Nevada, if I applied for public assistance, someone would call the media, and it would become a front page news story.

At that time, I had it in my head that I would move to Atlanta, Georgia. I had both friends and relatives there, and it seemed like a great city for a black woman to rebuild her life. So in 2007, and early 2008, I started sending job applications to Atlanta. I was invited to a few interviews, but at that time, the national economy was starting to spiral downward. Three employers called me back after the initial interviews to let me know that management had decided to not fill the positions due to budget constraints. While Atlanta seemed like it had great potential, it was apparent that every door of opportunity was closing.

Throughout this time, I'd share my job prospects with my mother, who, with my stepfather, had retired in San Antonio in 1996. My mom said, "Why don't you come home?" I just blew the suggestion off. Why would I ever go to San Antonio, Texas? I didn't even know anyone there other than my parents. I just wasn't feeling it.

As time went on; however, I knew in my spirit something had to give. I couldn't breathe in Las Vegas, and I had made up my mind that I never wanted to die there. I felt so strongly about that, in fact, that I had it put in my will. I had to go somewhere, and Atlanta wasn't bearing fruit.

One morning I was out walking and jogging. As I

always do, I had my iPod randomly playing my playlist of downloaded music. The song "Home" by American Idol contestant Chris Daughtry began to play. To say the song rocked me would be an understatement. It messed me up, especially the part about how these places and these faces are getting old.

Why couldn't I go home, especially after my mom had invited me? No reason other than pride and shame. I had left home at eighteen to go to Notre Dame and hadn't lived at home since. I was now forty-four years old. How could I move in with my folks, now in their late seventies? Pride and shame. How could I achieve things like becoming Miss Oregon, a city councilwoman, a county commissioner, a presidential appointee, etc., and now move back home? Pride and shame. Pride and shame. Pride and shame.

*My mom said, "Why don't you come home?"*

෨෨

Looking back over the course of my life, I think I allowed pride and shame this stronghold when I was a little girl and my parents divorced. It was probably a coping mechanism at the time because I had known of only one other family who had divorced parents. When it happened to me, I reacted by creating a strong exterior mask to cover the deep pain I felt. Now as an adult, I was again feeling deep hurt, but staying in place was not going to be an option. If I was going to have a healthy future anywhere, I had to release those strongholds I'd been carrying for about thirty-five years.

When I returned to my house after that walk, I made a decision that changed the course of my life. I decided I would go home, to the place where I belonged. I called my mother to tell her I had decided to move to San Antonio. I told her I would work out the details as to when. Her only request was that I not drive from Las Vegas to San Antonio by myself.

Two weeks after that revelation, my entire household was packed in a storage unit, and I was driving to Texas with my childhood friend, Leslie Cunningham. I had called Leslie shortly after I called my mom. Leslie lives in the Los Angeles area, and we became friends in Wüerzburg, Germany, when I was twelve and she was fourteen. She is probably the best friend I've ever had. I don't know many people who would just drop what's going on in their own lives to help a friend drive halfway across the country, but she got where I was coming from because God had also convicted her about overcoming her own pride and shame.

During the move, I had to ask for help from my former spouse. I had no desire to uproot my children because I didn't know if I would be staying in San Antonio for a month, a year, or a lifetime. With so much uncertainty in my life, I didn't want the uncertainty to impact my children. Although we have joint custody of our children, I told my ex that I would need the children to stay with him until the school year was finished.

I moved to my parents' home in a suburb of San Antonio named Converse on a street that has a weird French name, Voir Dire. I remember the first morning walk with my iPod after I moved to Voir Dire. I remember asking God, "What now? What now?" I didn't know what I would be doing for the rest of my life or why I was there or for how long. I just knew I was broke and totally dependent on my senior citizen parents. I also knew that whenever I felt bad about it, it was because of pride and shame. I had to press through those things.

It was while living on Voir Dire that I decided to apply to law school. I had been accepted to all of the Oregon law schools when I was Miss Oregon, but never attended. I have an older sister and brother who were both successful lawyers already. I questioned myself, "Did our family need a third?," but I began to accept that God had a plan for me that didn't have anything to do with my brother or sister's success. It was a plan to prosper me and to give me my own future and hope. During that time, I learned what Voir Dire means: "To speak the truth." It's also a legal term to describe the process of selecting a jury. As a trial lawyer today, I can tell you that selecting the jury is the most important part of a trial. The point was not lost on me that when I was able to be free of pride and shame, God literally took me to a street called Voir Dire.

God also showed me on Voir Dire that my parents needed me almost as much as I needed them. Although we are a blended family of eight children, no one lived in the same city as our parents until I moved to San Antonio. My parents no longer needed a house sitter when they traveled. I was there. There was even a time during that first year when both Ma and Sergeant Major were in casts—she had had surgery on her feet, and he had fallen at a church fish and fry—and neither could drive. I was able to drive them to their doctor appointments and to church.

I finally moved into graduate student housing during my second year of law school and then lived in my own apartment the year after. Even then, my parents were still close by, and that was a blessing to me. As an undergraduate at Notre Dame, my parents never could attend special functions such as Junior Parents' Weekend, but when I was a student at St. Mary's Law, they attended *every* function—every reception and every awards banquet. Part of the reason law school was so much fun was that my parents were in the same city and were such a part of my experience.

I could probably write an entire book on all the good that has happened to me in San Antonio. Today, I can't even imagine living in another city. I became a lawyer here. I'm writing this book here. I learned I was a pretty good professor here. I could go on and on.

San Antonio was named in honor of a Franciscan monk, Saint Anthony of Padua. I have read that he is the patron saint of lost things. So much that was lost in my life has been found in this city—peace, love, and hope, especially. I wouldn't have any of it if I hadn't released my pride and shame and moved.

Today, I share a lot more about myself than I ever have. I try to be transparent. I know a lot of people look up to me, and I want them to know that I have had personal struggles and have overcome some serious setbacks, just as they have. Until I let go of pride and shame, I never knew how much these things had shackled me. I never knew how liberating it would be to let it all go on Voir Dire.

During the spring semester of my first year in law school, I finally began sharing my life experiences with my classmates. At the "Break Rounds" event for first-year law students, the Board of Advocates, the student organization that organizes various moot court and mock trial competitions at the Law Center, makes an announcement. Most of the first year students were gathered there to find out if they would be among the top thirty-two teams advancing to the next rounds of competition. All first-year students are required to compete in the initial rounds,

*I let go of pride and shame.*

and that year the Moot Court competition had started with 130 two-member teams. Only thirty-two teams would "break," advancing to the next level in the competition. My team finished ninth out of 130 teams.

At the party, two of my classmates asked me, "Who *are* you?" They had been in my section and had observed me all year. As they put it, I had to have some kind of in-depth knowledge of government because of how I would volunteer to brief certain cases and appeared to have a strong grasp of procedural issues discussed in our various law classes. The time had come for me to "come clean" with my classmates. My pride and shame had evaporated enough, and the shackles had been unlocked. I told them I had been both a city councilwoman and a county commissioner.

A few days later, in my constitutional law class, I actually volunteered to brief the US Supreme Court case *Buckley v. Valeo*. The professor had asked for a volunteer, and I was the only person in the entire section to raise my hand. The word had already spread about my past among the eighty students in my section at that point. Another student told me after class that he'd Googled me and couldn't believe I actually had a Wikipedia page of my own. Frankly, that, too, had been a source of shame. However, my classmate both surprised and humored me with his response, "Dude, you're badass!"

That comment and my experiences for the remainder of my years in law school taught me that the generation behind mine, made up of the twenty- and thirty-something's, is a lot more forgiving and tolerant than the generation I grew up in. They tend to see the good over the bad in people. I'm grateful to have spent three years of my life with classmates who were primarily younger than me. Pride and shame can have such a stronghold and did for me, but coming clean to my classmates was a major turning point in seeing myself as God sees me. I am wonderfully and fearfully made. And yes, a badass!

Pride and shame can prevent us from claiming glorious rewards God intends for us to enjoy. Is there something you know God is calling you to do, but you cannot follow His lead because of pride and shame? Are you worried about what people think if you do the thing He wants you to do, like I was? Don't be! Answer to God, not to those who expect your actions to fit into their expectations of what you should do and be. God is the only one who matters.

*Coming clean to my classmates was a major turning point in seeing myself as God sees me.*

# Chapter 10

# Power of the Tithe

*Bring the whole tithe into the storehouse, that there may be food in my house. "Test me in this," says the LORD Almighty, "and see if I will not throw open the floodgates of heaven and pour out so much blessing that there will not be room enough to store it."*
—Malachi 3:10 (NIV)

lthough I had attended church regularly my entire life, I had never embraced the concept of tithing. I had heard the term before but never had taken the time to fully understand it until my God chase. Tithing means a tenth. It's accepting the truth that all things belong to God. To tithe is to return the first fruits of our labor back to Him, keeping 90 percent for ourselves.

Ironically, it was when I was flat broke and unemployed for eighteen months, drawing solely from unemployment checks that were but a fraction of what my monthly bills were, that I decided to test God as the scripture in Malachi challenged me to. I had absolutely no income, but I typically would have at least one dollar in my pocket. While I was still in Las Vegas and when I later moved to Texas, still having no income at all, I continued to tithe one dollar.

There was a teenager at ICLV who served as an usher, although he was confined to a wheelchair. His name was Sammy Lee. Despite his disability, it was obvious Sammy Lee had a servant's spirit. He was generous with his time. He greeted me and others with the biggest smile every Sunday. Unfortunately, he went home to the Lord before I left Las Vegas. I attended his funeral service. What I remembered most about that service was that his parents gave the church this oversized yellow crayon that was his piggy bank of sorts. The crayon stood about three feet tall and was filled with change. It was Sammy's life savings. Sammy's wish was for it to go to the church. After that service, I continued my tithing, but with a different heart. In the spirit of Sammy Lee, I gave joyfully.

When I moved to Texas and filed a Chapter 7 in 2008, one of the final matters involved with discharge was returning my car to the bank that had financed it. This happened in the summer of 2009, just weeks before I was to start law school. At that point, I had no transportation to school, which was thirty miles away from my parents' house.

One night, I had a conversation with God that basically went like this. "God, I don't have transportation. If you want me to be a lawyer, you're going to have to provide transportation to me." I'm not exaggerating when I say that about forty-eight hours later, I received a call from my youngest brother, Anthony. Anyone who knows this particular brother of mine knows that he never calls and he never returns calls. Looking down at the caller ID on my cell phone and seeing Anthony's name, my first thought was that he was having some kind of medical emergency.

As it turned out, it wasn't an emergency at all. Anthony called to say that one of his friends in Oregon had bought a new car and wasn't sure what he'd be doing with his old one, a little two-door economy Ford. Anthony said he'd told his friend I might be needing a car for law school and had asked him about selling it. The purpose of Anthony's call that day was to make certain whether or not I needed a car. I did, but in the back of my mind I was attempting to figure out how I'd pay for it when I didn't have a job. With hesitancy, I asked the one question I was dreading, "How much, Anthony?"

"He said he'd sell it to me for a buck, and I'll sell it to you for a buck."

One dollar. One dollar. One dollar. All that ran through my mind was all the Sundays I'd joyfully given one dollar. Now when I needed a serious breakthrough, God had provided the answer, and it was going to cost only one dollar. Anthony drove the car from Oregon to Las Vegas, and one of my mother's friends (again, provision provided) used her frequent-flyer miles to get me a one-way trip to Las Vegas so that I could drive the car back to

San Antonio. This one testimony made me a champion of tithing.

Tithing doesn't have to be about cash. I've found that when I give God the beginning of my day, I typically have a better day. I start out in the right frame of mind. I also try to give a portion of my law practice to pro bono cases. Every time I take on a client without compensation, I find I end up with three new paying clients.

*One dollar. All that ran through my mind was all the Sundays I'd joyfully given one dollar.*

Whenever the enemy tries to stir up fear over financial matters, I battle back with the reminders of all of the financial miracles God has brought me through. The quick answer to my desperate prayer for a vehicle in 2009, is especially reassuring, but that wasn't all. God did it again by helping me pay for my bar review course and to be able to study for the bar exam for seven weeks without needing to work, even part-time. God is my Jehovah Jireh. All He asks of me and anyone else is that we test Him. I personally intend to test him a lot with my time, my talents, and my treasure.

He wants your time, talents, and treasure, too. If you have never tithed, or have never done so regularly, try to make it a priority, even if you feel that you are already having difficulty making ends meet. Being obedient in this area will please God, and He will reward you for it. Give as you are able, and do so joyfully. The New Testament says, "Each one must give as he has decided in his heart, not reluctantly or under compulsion, for God loves a cheerful giver" (2 Corinthians 9:7, ESV).

# Chapter 11

# The Blessings of
# Manasseh and Ephraim

*What if the thousand sleepless nights are what it takes to*
*know You're near*
*What if trials of this life are Your mercies in disguise?*
—"Blessings" by Laura Story

A powerful experience for me of late is that God's been showing me the "rest of the story" of some of the Bible stories that really sustained me during my molting season. For example, for the longest time, I would read over and over again the story of the three Hebrew boys, Meshach, Shadrach, and Abednego. I had focused for years on the fact that God had joined them in the fire and that they had come out without the smell of smoke. Just that part of the story inspired me, but one Sunday, my pastor, Duane Lowe, preached what came after

the Hebrew boys got out of the fire. For some reason—
perhaps I just wasn't ready to hear it—I had never got past
the part where they got out of the fire, but that Sunday, I
was finally able to receive the rest of the story.
Nebuchadnezzar, the very king who had thrown them into
the fire, *promoted* them. "Huh? How did I miss that part?"

A similar thing happened to me while delving deeper
into the story of Joseph in the book of Genesis. Joseph
had been betrayed by his brothers and sold into slavery in
Egypt. Genesis 50:20 had, in many ways, become the story
of my life. Primarily, it was what Joseph said to his
brothers when they recognized that the governor of
Egypt, whom they needed for help, was the same little
brother they had sold out. Joseph said to his brothers, "You
intended to harm me, but God intended it for good. He
brought me to this position so I could save the lives of
many people" (Genesis 50:20, NLT).

It was not until 2011, when I got a Christmas card
from Pastors Paul and Denise Goulet of ICLV, that I was
led to go back a few chapters, specifically to chapter 41
of Genesis, and reflect on the significance of the two
children who had been born to Joseph and his wife,
Asenath. The verses state that before the seven-year famine
that Joseph had interpreted from Pharaoh's dream, he had
two sons. The first son was Manasseh, whose name means
"God made me forget all my troubles and everyone in my
father's family" (Genesis 41:51, NLT). The second son was
Ephraim, whose name means "God has made me fruitful
in this land of my grief" (Genesis 41:52, NLT).

Many years had gone by for Joseph to reach that place. What was significant to me reading about Manasseh and Ephraim is that through a process of healing and the passage of time, you will come to a place where the deep, painful memories will subside. Only God can make that happen. Drinking can't take it away. Prescription drugs can't take it away. Promiscuity can't take it away. Only God can. And in my experience, you really can't move forward until you can forget all your troubles. It doesn't mean that they are erased as if they never happened; they just no longer become the emotional roadblock or stronghold they once were. You move on.

I also believe sincerely in Ephraim. It was no coincidence, at least to me, that Ephraim was the second son. Once we are able to forget all the troubles of the past, it is possible to be fruitful in the very place that was the source of the trouble and pain. I have seen this played out in so many of my friends' lives, as well as my own. I have a friend who was kidnapped and forced into sex trafficking as a teenager. Today she helps women get out of prostitution. I have a friend who lost a child in an automobile accident many years ago who today is an elementary school counselor. Being charged with crimes was a tremendous source of pain for me in 2007, but today I'm a successful criminal defense lawyer and I'm writing this book to help others overcome their own painful experiences.

Many times, I would read chapter 42 of the book of Job. When I take the story of Joseph and the story of Job together, it serves as a reminder that God can and will take our painful experiences and restore the things that were lost. He doesn't return you to the place where you were

*Being charged with crimes was a tremendous source of pain for me in 2007, but today I'm a successful criminal defense lawyer.*

ॐॐ

when the painful experience took place; He always gives you *more*. Joseph received more than what was in the dream he had shared with his brothers. His two sons are proof of that. Job received more land, more cattle, more children, and more everything.

God gave them both so much that they both had the same ending. They died full. God has already given me so much back. I've decided I'm not going to try and box God in. I'm going to just let God be God. The only request I've

made of Him is to let me die full, like Joseph and Job. I want to leave this life full and I want everyone reading this book to die full. The message Manasseh and Ephraim teach is a huge part of achieving that fullness for all of us.

# Chapter 12

# My Patmos

*He will cover you with his feathers,*
*and under his wings you will find refuge;*
*his faithfulness will be your shield and rampart.*
*— Psalm 91:4 NIV*

It truly has been a seven-year season. Although I had friends and family who were in my life during this time, in many ways it truly was the first time in my life when I felt it was all about me and God and no one else. There are so many stories in the Bible about how God showed up in powerful ways when the subject of the story was apart from the world, and the person found herself or himself alone with God. One of the most powerful stories for me is that of the apostle John.

John, one of the twelve handpicked by Jesus, was banished by the Emperor Domitian to an island called Patmos, a small Greek island located in the Aegean Sea.

Translated from Greek to English, Patmos means "my killing." John had been with Jesus in the Garden of Gethsemane, and he had witnessed Jesus's crucifixion. Many accounts of the crucifixion state that it was John to whom Jesus entrusted to look after his mother, Mary. John; his brother, James; and Peter were the only three apostles who witnessed the transfiguration of Jesus. It is clear that God entrusted John with much.

James and Peter both died violently, but Emperor Domitian banished John to not only a certain death, but a death in solitude. It was in this place of his killing, his isolation, and inside a cave called Apocalypse, that God found John. God spoke to him in such a powerful way that the message became what we know today as the book of Revelation. John penned the following:

> I, John, both your brother and companion in the tribulation and kingdom and patience of Jesus Christ, was on the island that is called Patmos for the word of God and for the testimony of Jesus Christ. I was in the Spirit on the Lord's Day, and I heard behind me a loud voice, as of a trumpet, saying, "I am the Alpha and the Omega, the First and the Last," and, "What you see, write in a book and send it to the seven churches which are in Asia: to Ephesus, to Smyrna, to Pergamos, to Thyatira, to Sardis, to Philadelphia, and to Laodicea" (Revelation 1:9–11, NIV).

It is important to point out the difference between self-inflicted isolation and mandated isolation. Self-inflicted isolation is dangerous. It's when you've isolated yourself from family, church, people who care about you, and things and situations that can only help you grow in your spiritual walk. When we're not connected to anyone through our own choosing, we're like tumbleweeds, just rolling around in the desert, not knowing where we'll ultimately land. We don't have direction or purpose. Self-inflicted isolation may also come from circumstances in our lives. Perhaps like Jacob, in the Bible, it comes about because of our own shenanigans and shortcomings.

Mandated isolation is different. It's when God sets you in a place where it's just you and Him. The purpose of mandated isolation is to give you revelation. You may see the isolation not as a blessing, but as a curse. However, in the quietness of the times when it's just you and God, you will receive the greatest impartation of the power and promises God has to offer. In that isolation, God can show up and reveal Himself in a way like no other. I, like John, had to be obedient to God and write about all the things he revealed to me while on my personal Patmos.

I specifically remember one night at the beginning of my Patmos that I had given up the will to live. This was before I left Las Vegas. I was isolated. I felt like a leper. I felt rejected. I had rampant thoughts running through my mind of buying a gun and ending my life, but I started thinking about my children and a future stigma of having a mother who blew her brains out. After that, my next thought was carbon monoxide poisoning. Perhaps if I just turned the car on in the garage, I could just fall asleep into the next life, but I started, just like I did with the gun, to overthink it.

One night, out of desperation, I asked God to do it. I wanted Him to end my life. I knew that if God was the Creator who breathed life into men and women, He certainly was capable of ending my breathing. I told God that the people said I was worthless, washed up, a liar, and had nothing good to contribute to this world. It really was that basic and simple, as I saw it. I pleaded with God, "If these news reporters and other Lynette haters are right, take my life, God; kill me." I was convinced that I had no value in 2007. I really believed it.

Most people I tell this story to laugh when I say, "I woke up the next morning." It was not a funny matter to me at all. I was so desperate, and it was my hope I wouldn't wake up. I was at Patmos, and people are sent to Patmos to die.

The first person I called was one of my friends from ICLV who is still one of my closest friends today. I called her because she had also contemplated suicide at one time in her life. She had been a prostitute on the Las Vegas strip for many years until one night, one of her best friends was killed by her john. That was a Patmos moment for my friend. She already owned a gun and put it to her head. She had told this story to me and to so many others through the years. In her desperation, she asked God to show up, and it was there, alone in a hotel room, that God began to revel to her the life she would have away from prostitution, off of drugs, as a wife, as someone who'd be helping other young women get out of prostitution. All my friend said to me when I called her was "Don't do it, girl. God has so much for you." I've always thanked God for bringing a friend into my life whose struggle and testimony would help me in saving my own life. I thank my friend for her own testimony and for her unconditional love and support, even as I write this book.

As I type the words in this final chapter, I find myself once again in isolation. My current husband and I have struggled throughout the course of our marriage. Literally a few days ago, he insisted that I leave his house where I have lived since we tied the knot. Once again, I find myself in isolation not knowing how the story of this relationship will unfold. However, in my human sadness of not having the kind of marriage relationship I had prayed about, God continually shows me that I must surrender Michael and our marriage to Him. I don't know how this story will end. I only know how *my* story will end and that it will be victorious. The only thing I can do on Patmos is, like I did before, die to myself and let God be God. The enemy wants us to take our life in the literal sense, but God wants us to die to the solutions of this world and to put our full trust in Him. It is so true, as Francis of Assisi wrote it, that only in dying do we receive eternal life.

Today, I know that seasons of isolation are a blessing. I look at times like now as a tremendous opportunity for

God to reveal things to me in deeper ways. Patmos isn't a life sentence. It's a place where God can move and speak profoundly to you so that what you learn there can be shared with others for His glory.

*I don't know how this story will end. I only know how my story will end and that it will be victorious.*

I didn't sit down and write this book for the seven churches. If it ends up there, it definitely is a God thing. Like John, I had to just sit and write about all the things God showed me when I became the rejected stone, when I died. That is, God resurrected a woman who strives every day to see things as Jesus would, who believes she can heal the sick and spread the Good News, and who, most important for me, received a heart transplant. The truth that God showed me on Patmos was that I once lived in a world of "us" and "them" until God made me one of them. Now I know there's only "us." There is *no* "them."

I also got "souled out" during this spiritual journey. I heard the same voice that John heard announcing, "I am the Alpha and the Omega, the First and the Last" (Revelation 22:13, NIV). No one can turn me around from this truth. My tribulations caused me to grow deep roots of faith. I'm like a tree planted by a river; I can't be moved off Jesus.

I hope this book will help strengthen those who have felt beaten down and rejected. Having been there, I can tell you with all my heart and soul that you have value in God's eyes. What God has in store for you is so much bigger than you can even imagine. Your best days are in front of you.

*If you can learn to see things through spiritual eyes, like John, you will receive great revelations.*

By the way, John didn't die on the island of Patmos. He died peacefully in Ephesus at a ripe old age. Domitian might have had an agenda, but God turned that situation around for His glory. I am seeing this play out in my life and in the lives of so many people I know. It will also play out in *your* life. If you can learn to see things through spiritual eyes, like John, you will receive great revelations. I receive them not because I'm holier or more righteous than anyone. I'm not. I've messed up, but I accept I am God's treasure and not only me, but so are my estranged husbands. Even in the uncertainties of life, from family to career, I receive revelation when I'm alone in His presence and am willing to die to myself.

Whatever season you may be in right now, may El-Shaddai, the almighty God of peace, hope, and love, be with you always. And know that there is a lawyer/freedom minister in San Antonio praying God's will for your life right now.

### THE END

# *Epilogue*

The devil lost that wager in Sin City. God prevailed. Not only did His servant, Lynette, grow in her faith, she became even bolder because she knew who had delivered her from the snare.

As Lynette prayed, and continues to pray, for her friends and others, the Lord began restoring her. The story continues to unfold with more—more faith, more friends, more experiences, and more opportunities.

In the end, God promises the same reward for her—and for you—that he gave to Job, Joseph, and all who put their trust in Him. She will die peaceful and content, free of the guilt, shame, and unforgiveness that once imprisoned her.

# CONTINUE THE PURSUIT

If you believe in the message of this book and would like to help in getting this important message out, please consider taking part by:

• Writing about *Finding God in Sin City* on your blog, Twitter, Instagram and Facebook page.

• Suggesting *Finding God in Sin City* to friends and send them to the book's website Flygirlbooks.com.

• When you're in a bookstore, ask them if they carry the book. The book is available through all major distributors, so any bookstore that does not have it in stock can easily order it.

• Encourage your book club to read *Finding God in Sin City*.

• Writing a positive review on www.amazon.com

• Invite Lynette Boggs Quintanilla to speak at an event by visiting Flygirlbooks.com.

• Purchasing additional copies to give away as gifts.